Deleuze Studies
Volume 7 Number 2 2013
Deleuze and Philosophical Practice

Edited by Guillaume Collett, Masayoshi Kosugi and Chryssa Sdrolia

T0317935

Edinburgh University Press

Subscription rates for 2013

Four issues per year, published in February, May, August and November

		Tier	UK	RoW	N. America
Institutions	Print & online	1	£120.00	£130.50	$233.00
		2	£150.00	£160.50	$284.00
		3	£187.50	£198.00	$348.00
		4	£225.00	£235.50	$412.00
		5	£255.00	£265.50	$463.00
	Online	1	£102.00	£102.00	$173.00
		2	£127.50	£127.50	$217.00
		3	£159.00	£159.00	$270.00
		4	£191.00	£191.00	$325.00
		5	£216.50	£216.50	$368.00
Individuals	Print		£40.00	£45.00	$81.00
	Online		£40.00	£40.00	$73.00
	Print & online		£50.00	£57.00	$104.00
	Back issues/ single copies		£11.00	£12.50	$22.00
Students	Student Print		£24.00	£27.00	$48.50
	Student Online		£24.00	£24.00	$43.00
	Student Print & Online		£30.00	£34.00	$61.00

How to order

Subscriptions can be accepted for complete volumes only. Print prices include packing and airmail for subscribers in North America and surface postage for subscribers in the Rest of the World. Volumes back to the year 2000 (where applicable) are included in online prices. Print back volumes will be charged at
the current volume subscription rate.

All orders must be accompanied by the correct payment. You can pay by cheque in Pound Sterling or US Dollars, bank transfer, Direct Debit or Credit/Debit Card. The individual rate applies only when a subscription is paid for with a personal cheque, credit card or bank transfer.

To order using the online subscription form, please visit www.euppublishing.com/page/dls/subscribe

Alternatively you may place your order by telephone on +44 (0)131 650 6207, fax on +44 (0)131 662 3286 or email to journals@eup.ed.ac.uk using your Visa or Mastercard credit card. Don't forget to include the expiry date of your card, the security number (three digits on the reverse of the card) and the address that the card is registered to.

Please make your cheque payable to Edinburgh University Press Ltd. Sterling cheques must be drawn on a UK bank account.

If you would like to pay by bank transfer or Direct Debit, contact us at journals@eup.ed.ac.uk and we will provide instructions.

Advertising

Advertisements are welcomed and rates are available on request, or by consulting our website at www.euppublishing.com. Advertisers should send their enquiries to the Journals Marketing Manager at the address above.

Contents

Editors' Acknowledgements

We would very much like to thank the following people who acted as referees: Simon Duffy, Gavin Rae, Nathan Widder, Claudia Mongini, Brian W. Smith, Iain MacKenzie, Emma Ingala, Dorothea Olkowski, Edward Willatt, Caroline Williams and Gerald Cipriani.

Special thanks to Marjorie Gracieuse, Jean-Claude Dumoncel, David Savat, Ian Buchanan and Les Back.

Deleuze Studies 7.2 (2013): v
DOI: 10.3366/dls.2013.0099
© Edinburgh University Press
www.euppublishing.com/dls

Editorial Introduction: For a Transdisciplinary Practice of Thought

Guillaume Collett University of Kent

Masayoshi Kosugi and Chryssa Sdrolia Goldsmiths, University of London

All the articles presented in this issue have their origin in the conference 'Deleuze, Philosophy, Transdisciplinarity', which took place in London in February 2012 and which the present editors organised. The key question that the conference sought to address and around which the present issue revolves is the following: How are we to understand philosophy's relation to the various thought processes and practices of other disciplines in the work of Gilles Deleuze? The necessity of asking this question is to be found in a difficulty we perceive to exist in the tendency for an interdisciplinary mode of knowledge production. As the desire to bring together a multitude of different research fields grows, particularly in the humanities, it has also become harder to compare and conjoin them without a certain perplexity arising as to how the different protocols and traditions of thought are to intersect.

Our turn to Deleuze is precisely motivated by his distinctive take on the problem, which we will here articulate as 'transdisciplinarity'.[1] We take our cue from the blurb of the French edition of *What Is Philosophy?*, which reads: 'Philosophy is not interdisciplinary'.[2] This might be taken to harbour a tension. After all, it is known that Deleuze had long insisted on the essential relation between philosophy and other disciplines. His work has been explicitly and on numerous occasions praised for having advocated the necessity of breaking through traditional disciplinary boundaries and can be rightly described as one of the boldest instances of Continental philosophy. As Isabelle Stengers notes, Deleuze's thought has been associated with 'the affirmation

Deleuze Studies 7.2 (2013): 157–168
DOI: 10.3366/dls.2013.0100
© Edinburgh University Press
www.euppublishing.com/dls

of productive connections, the creation of deterritorialising processes escaping fixed identities, transgressing the power of exclusive disjunction that is the either/or alternatives, such as, for instance, doing either science or philosophy' (Stengers 2005: 151). The same can be said of Deleuze's engagement with other traditions. Besides the sciences, from *Difference and Repetition* ([1968] 1994) to *A Thousand Plateaus* ([1980] 1988) and *Cinema 1* and *2* ([1983] 1986; [1985] 1989), philosophy is actively shown to thrive on a multitude of connections with the arts, technology and the social sciences. Indeed, we may identify a strong *centrifugal* movement in his writings – intensified in some ways after his collaboration with Félix Guattari – by which philosophy is audaciously extended towards other disciplines. Expressed and practised as a logic of the 'and', this transversal way of thinking emerges as a choice, as a particular ethic of doing philosophy, and its stakes are laid out clearly: contrary to an image of thought as disinterested 'contemplation' that would close up on itself to induce a return to pre-established canons, for Deleuze philosophy must open itself up to other practices of knowledge production. Such an opening is not only possible but also necessary if philosophy is to be divested of a false and detrimental aura of contemplative universality and mastery over other modes of thought.

Yet at the same time that this opening is affirmed and consciously practised against the pitfalls of mere 'contemplation', in his late work with Guattari, Deleuze's philosophy appears to be defined by a *centripetal* and self-restricting movement, which delimits and breaks connections. Compared with the profusion of adventurous links animating previous works, *What is Philosophy?* might be taken to promote a surprisingly conservative picture, with philosophy trying to establish itself and its own methods in contradistinction to what it is not. In the book, philosophy, science and art are indeed considered apart from one another, each shown to create through its own mode, to have its own outside (non-philosophy, non-science, non-art) and to correspond to different disciplinary planes of immanence, reference and composition, respectively. 'The three planes, along with their elements, are irreducible' (Deleuze and Guattari [1991] 1994: 216). Philosophy produces concepts; science produces functions; art produces affects and percepts. And if they can be said to 'interfere' (Deleuze and Guattari [1991] 1994: 216–18) with each other, this interference proceeds through their individual means: out of a function or an affect and percept, philosophy can make a concept; out of an affect and percept or a concept, science can make a function; out of a concept or a function, art can make an affect and percept. The point is repeated in the American preface to *Difference and Repetition* written in 1994, only three years after the publication of *What Is Philosophy?*:

> A philosophical concept can never be confused with a scientific function or an artistic construction, but finds itself in affinity with these in this or that domain of science or style of art. The scientific or artistic content of a philosophy may be very elementary, since it is not obliged to advance art or science, but it can advance itself only by forming properly philosophical concepts from a given function or construction. (Deleuze [1968] 1994: xvi)

As Deleuze himself asserts in this particular instance, when he strays into mathematical and biological territory to make concepts out of the functions of 'differentiation' and 'differenciation', the movement that enables him to connect with those practices abides by certain disciplinary protocols, restrictions and rules. The differences between disciplines are not to be ignored.

Is there a contradiction between the two movements? Are we presented, as Alain Badiou indicates, with an imperative to choose, as it were, between two Deleuzes, one 'radical', the other 'temperate' (Badiou [1997] 2000: 9)? More specifically to our problematic, are we faced with the impossibility of the cross-fertilisation of disciplines and with the surreptitious re-establishment of boundaries? Deleuze hints at the answer as early as 1972 in an interview with Catherine Backès-Clément: 'I'm interested in the way a page of writing flies off in all directions and at the same time closes right up on itself like an egg' (Deleuze [1990] 1995: 14). We can see from this quotation that the situation is more complex than the one implied by our previously staged dualism between a promiscuous and a classical way of philosophising. The centrifugal and centripetal movements cannot be taken to cancel out one another, nor can they be said to have emerged at different points in Deleuze's career. On the contrary, it becomes clear that they have always been complementary, the two components of a single movement, with each component articulated sometimes with more, sometimes with less emphasis. One finds this in *Difference and Repetition*, where the practice of transcendental empiricism frees the transcendental from the a priori and the conditions of possible experience, reconstituting it on the back of a disciplinary pluralism spanning the arts and sciences. The latter are now un/grounded in a problematic transcendental field no longer reducible to philosophy itself. But is this also the case in *What is Philosophy?* The question must be answered positively. For at the end of the book, the separation of disciplines is simultaneously co-articulated with the appeal to a point of divergence that is nevertheless common to all of them. This is the brain, the '*junction* – not the unity – *of the three planes*', which, being a determinate cluster of neighbourhoods, a 'complex both of horizontal connections and of vertical integrations reacting on one another', is the condition of transdisciplinarity itself (Deleuze and Guattari [1991] 1994: 208). It is at this level that the disciplines are treated non-hierarchically. The brain reveals, or rather, it practises, a subtle art of 'interferences' that can proceed extrinsically, intrinsically or in a non-localisable way. Accordingly, there can be connections proceeding unilaterally and through individual means; or connections that slip from one plane to another and that cannot be safely claimed by either; or connections that pertain to each discipline's relation to its own outside. But there is another level of equality; for through the brain, the planes of immanence, composition and reference are also plunged into chaos where they are finally confronted with the impossibility of their distinction: 'concepts, sensations, and functions become undecidable, at the same time as philosophy, art and science become indiscernible, as if they shared the same shadow that extends itself across their different nature and constantly accompanies them' (218). If *What Is Philosophy?* puts forth a unique take on transdisciplinarity, it is because it advocates a relation between disciplines that is more than a simple separation.

From this perspective, the 'separation' of philosophy, art and science is not a prescription, a parting of the ways or a comment on the impossibility of a cross-fertilisation of disciplines. Above all, it is a cautionary gesture. For the path to creative connections is strewn with the dangers of 'communication' manifested as the tendency of theorising discourses to assume the voice of 'common sense' in order to dictate to others how they should know what they know. We may stage an imaginary dialogue between Foucault and Deleuze at this point:

> But, then, what is philosophy today – philosophical activity, I mean – if it is not the critical work that thought brings to bear on itself? In what does it consist, if not in the endeavour to know how and to what extent it might be possible to think differently, instead of legitimating what is already known? There is always something ludicrous in philosophical discourse when it tries, from the outside, to dictate to others, to tell them where their truth is and how to find it, or when it works up a case against them in the language of naïve positivity. But it is entitled to explore what might be changed, in its own thought, through the practice of a knowledge that is foreign to it. The 'essay' – which should be understood as the assay or test by which, in

the game of truth, one undergoes changes, and not just as the simplistic appropriation of others for the purpose of communication – is the living substance of philosophy, at least if we assume that philosophy is still what it was in times past, i.e. an 'ascesis,' askesis, an exercise of oneself in the activity of thought. (Foucault [1984] 1985: 8–9)

For many people, philosophy is something which is not 'made', but is pre-existent, ready-made in a prefabricated sky. However, philosophical theory is itself a practice, just as much as its object. It is no more abstract than its object. It is a practice of concepts, and it must be judged in the light of the other practices with which it interferes. (Deleuze [1985] 1989: 280)

The second quote can be taken as a reply to the first, since Deleuze indeed read an extract from *The Use of Pleasure* as his eulogy for Foucault. Published the following year, *Cinema 2* expresses precisely that mode of thinking which Foucault describes. Deleuze presents us with a philosophy that lives by interfering with, and simultaneously rendering itself sensitive to, something 'foreign' – to a cinematic, scientific or other way of thinking – which it cannot claim for its own but which enables philosophy to evolve as a practice of concepts. It is at this level of philosophy as practice that the apparent contradiction between the two movements we staged and the ambivalence of *What is Philosophy?* need to be thought: *qua* distinct 'modes of Ideation', disciplines are all *practices*, each no more or less abstract than the other. The point is not for philosophy to stop looking outside itself for inspiration or to lay claim to superiority over other disciplines. The point is that the practice of transdisciplinarity needs to proceed with care. If, returning to *A Thousand Plateaus*, Deleuze and Guattari tell us that the plane of consistency is always 'constructed [...], in very different social formations through very different assemblages (perverse, artistic, scientific, mystical, political)', the question nevertheless remains one of caution: 'whether the pieces can fit together, and at what price' (Deleuze and Guattari [1980] 1988: 157). For the stakes are never purely theoretical but always also practical. In *A Thousand Plateaus*, the construction of the plane of consistency always involves the assembling of flows of desire, the practical implications of which are extended into Deleuze's last published work where 'pure immanence' is twinned with an impersonal practice, 'A LIFE' (Deleuze [1995] 2001: 27).

It is at this crossroads of practices of thought that the political value of a transdisciplinary practice of interference becomes manifest. That the three disciplines can 'interbreed' but claim the offspring respecting the conceptual, functional or affective-perceptive method of conception is not a limitation but a warning against the relativistic application of concepts across fields. Interference, the practice of transversing boundaries, needs to proceed with care. Of course, as we have seen above, we are not speaking of a method that functions as a final end or as a programmatic perspective given once and for all. A discipline may create something unexpected, if, as we saw, the interference proceeds subtly. The only requirement, then, is that the connection between disciplines be constantly reinvented, respecting their distinct specificities while being able to induce the new without claiming mastery or assuming power over one another. Above all, what is at stake is an understanding of transdisciplinarity as a practice capable of bypassing the facile opposition between contemplation and action, theory and praxis.[3]

*

All articles contained in this issue may be considered to express this single centrifugal–centripetal movement in terms of the problematic of transdisciplinarity as practice. In doing so, they aspire to shed light on a crucial aspect of Deleuze's practice of concepts as the condition for the articulation of a philosophy that will be 'no more abstract than its object' (Deleuze [1985] 1989: 280) but, strictly speaking, a practical or ethico-aesthetic experiment, to use a Guattarian notion, always in the process of reconfiguring itself.

   In 'Deleuze Challenges Kolmogorov on a Calculus of Problems', Jean-Claude Dumoncel reveals the character of Deleuze's philosophy as a 'practice of problems' by reviving the latter's encounter with mathematical intuitionism on the contested territory of the Leibnizian *Calculemus*. The article proceeds by tackling Deleuze's transformation of logico-mathematical structures as conducive to the very conceptualisation of the 'problem' in properly metaphysical terms. Beginning with a review of Kolmogorov's constructive logic, Dumoncel discusses the implications of the Deleuzian decision to liberate the principle of the excluded middle from the epistemological focus of the standard propositional calculus and restore it into an ontological '*law of being and becoming*'. At stake in this act is the articulation of the relation between the calculus of problems and propositional calculus as a nuanced but non-hierarchical relation of 'discriminating power'. According to this power, Dumoncel argues, the calculus of problems emerges as being able to '[detect] *differences* in the propositional calculus'. But this can only happen 'on condition that [the calculus of problems] is (morphologically) *identical* to [propositional calculus]'. Paradoxically, it is precisely '*because* the symbolic formulas of the calculus of problems, literally taken, are *indiscernible* from the corresponding formulas in the propositional calculus' that difference can be detected by the repetition of the logical rules of the excluded middle on a metaphysical level. With this premise, the article goes on to plot a meticulous trail of conceptual connections, including the role of Leibnizian *themes*, Peircean *rhemes*, Hilbert's *Aristide* and Spinoza's parallelism at work in the metaphysicalisation of the propositional calculus into a calculus of problems. Principal among the latter is the subtle interference between philosophy and mathematics as exemplified by the encounter between Deleuze and Lautman. Deleuze is shown to engage with a Lautmanian dialectics in order to reveal the Idea as the extra-propositional and extra-philosophical plane that is differently actualised in logic, mathematics and philosophy but remains irreducible to them. The result of this second connection is brought to bear upon the nature of philosophical thought as one that, through a calculus of problems, takes for its object the very practice of concept creation as fundamentally transdisciplinary.

Daniela Voss's article 'Deleuze's Third Synthesis of Time' focuses on Deleuze's theory of time and especially the enigmatic character of the so-called 'third synthesis' by drawing attention to a series of extrinsically interfering philosophical, dramaturgical and mathematical lines that inform it. In the article, the dynamics of the conceptualisation of the static synthesis of the future is seen as driven by the notion of the 'cut'. Working her way through detailed readings of Kant's pure form of time, Hölderlin's 'caesura' and Dedekind's theory of continuity, Voss's thesis is that Deleuze's interest in the 'cut' is threefold: the 'cut' allows a static and purely ideal definition of continuity; it induces a break from empirical definitions of time as flow; and it permits the distribution of past and future affairs in a linear yet non-identical way. The three strands are then intercepted and bent through a Nietzschean lens. With the aid of the concept of the eternal return and its (Klossowskian) demand that whatever returns return as different and new, as simulacrum, Deleuze is then shown to achieve nothing less than a novel theory of the subject as non-identical to itself and multiple, always in the process of becoming. Deleuze's third synthesis of time presents us 'not simply an a priori subjective form, but an a priori and a-subjective static synthesis of a multiplicity of temporal series', immanent to the process of de/subjectivation. Yet the 'cut' here is not described as a means to articulate or simply 'contemplate' the possibility of an a-subjective a priori. As Voss argues, the 'cut' is first and foremost the means with which to engage with the untimely a-subjective field as a practice of thought, which immanently refashions Deleuze himself *as* political subject *in* the present and qualifies his way of philosophising as one of 'cutting theories together'. In fact, the article concludes, this is where the proper meaning of 'thought as heterogenesis' is to be found. By interfering with other modes of Ideation, such as mathematics and drama, Deleuze is able to invoke a 'becoming-other' of the subject that is first and foremost a logic of transdisciplinarity where thought exercises and expresses itself in heterogeneity.

Éric Alliez's article 'Ontology of the Diagram and Biopolitics of Philosophy: A Research Programme on Transdisciplinarity', uses the diagram to both develop a genealogy of and critically engage with Deleuze's and Deleuze and Guattari's practices of transdisciplinarity, culminating in an equally biopolitical and artistic critique of philosophy. The article examines how under the influence of Guattari, Deleuze extracts from Foucault in the mid-1970s a 'revolutionary diagram from which are derived both a new way of doing and a new way of speaking'. This is fleshed out in *A Thousand Plateaus* in terms of a constructivism of desire. Alliez's key proposition in the first part of his article is that the 'political plane of consistency' of the diagram – its complete immanence to the socio-political field and thus its capacity to construct it – must always be 'explicat[ed] and complicat[ed]' as '*Art and politics*'. The lines of flight or points of mutation lying between or prior to formed strata (or structures) excavated by Deleuze and Guattari's new practice of the diagram are also always, for Alliez, sensible signs open to artistic experimentation and creation. Thus, art is never 'an end in itself' but always a biopolitical practice (the construction of vital flows of desire). To explain how this in turn leads to a biopolitical critique of philosophy, the second part of the article charts the historical development of the Deleuzian and Guattarian concept of diagram out of Deleuze's transcendental empiricism and engagement with structuralism in the 1960s. While structuralism sought to establish a transdisciplinary conception of structure capable of opposing the 'theoretical primacy of philosophy', Alliez considers that Deleuze's key innovation in 'How Do We Recognise Structuralism?' was to fold structuralism *back* onto philosophy. This folding gives way to a 'new transcendental philosophy' literally turned inside-out by its internal reliance on other disciplines and practices for its ideational and sensible content. Alliez shows that it was thanks to Guattari that Deleuze could fully break with structuralism and realise its transdisciplinary outlook, by identifying the idealising 'operational closure' or 'disciplinary regulation' of structure with the internal limits of the capitalist system they sought to critique. The anti-structuralist outside of capital (and State philosophy) is therefore understandable, for Alliez, as both 'the politics of thought and politics inside thought' and '*Art after Philosophy*'.

For Deleuze, along with Guattari, politics as such is not categorically singled out as an autonomous mode of 'Ideation' like those of philosophy, science and art, respectively. Rather, politics assigns itself the form of transversal 'collective creations' or 'becomings', which cross disciplinary territorialities and hence cannot be localised in specific regions or groups of activities. Then what are the precise nature and the end of such politics? In 'Who Are Our Nomads Today?: Deleuze's Political Ontology and the Revolutionary Problematic', Craig Lundy seeks to explore and clarify these questions by elaborating upon another question posed as a political imperative by Deleuze in 1972, 'we must ask: who are our nomads today?' (Deleuze 2004: 260). For Lundy, this question demands that we turn to the ontological basis behind the conceptual distinction between the State and the nomad, as well as to Deleuze and Guattari's seemingly dualistic deployments of terms such as smooth/striated, as presented in *A Thousand Plateaus*. The view he offers is that such dualisms are ultimately rooted in Deleuze's long-sustained engagements with Henri Bergson's distinction between two types of multiplicities (of degree and of kind) and this distinction in fact serves as the ontological foundation of their political philosophy *tout court*. The lesson for politics he draws from the Bergsonian distinction allows him to reconfigure the seemingly dualistic definition of the nomad so that it is not dualistically opposed to the State. Rather, the nomad is defined in terms of a topological triad that supposes the 'second force of nomadism' placed in-between two kinds of multiplicities here transposed onto the polarity of State/nomad, a polarity that is initially established in an absolute manner. There are thus two nomads: the nomad conceived vis-à-vis the State and the nomad in-between the State and the nomad. The answer to the first question, 'who are today's nomads?' is thus answered behind our backs, for asking the question itself is part of philosophy as practice of thought.

In '"What Is Called Thinking?": When Deleuze Walks Along Heideggerian Paths', Benoît Dillet explores the complex relation between Deleuze and Heidegger in their respective formulations of 'thinking' as a political problem. While it is well known that Deleuze explicitly distanced himself from Heidegger's 'ontological Difference' in *Difference and Repetition*, Dillet argues that there is a more profound affinity between them with respect to their common thesis on thinking as a political problem. Dillet points out that when Deleuze repeatedly writes 'we are not yet thinking', he is referring to the same pronouncement made by Heidegger, and to the specific ways in which the latter called for an understanding of what thinking involves in his 1951–2 lectures entitled 'What Is Called Thinking?'. Dillet, drawing on Zourabichvili's take on Deleuze's political thought, argues that Deleuze's conception of thinking as an involuntary practice comes close to Heidegger's conception of thinking as 'releasement', which requires an unwillingness that simultaneously points to and withdraws from what calls for thinking. However, on the question regarding who, or better which discipline, has access to thought, the two thinkers are considered by Dillet to differ sharply. While for Heidegger, '[a]ll sciences are grounded in philosophy, but not *vice versa*', Deleuze, on the other hand, grants all disciplines full rights and power to ground themselves and to reflect upon their own 'supra-historical' foundations without relying on philosophy to do so. In short, while Heidegger draws a hierarchical picture of 'thinking' with philosophy sitting on top of all sciences, Deleuze 'democratises' thinking and sees it as equally capable of being accessed by all disciplines, albeit in their own particular ways. This openness of thought to disciplines other than philosophy is exemplified by Deleuze's work on cinema. Far from requiring philosophy to think on behalf of it, cinema is fully capable of thought in its own right, and it resists stupidity just as much as philosophy and science do.

Notes

1. We borrow the term 'transdisciplinarity' from the research programme currently underway in the Centre for Research in Modern European Philosophy at Kingston University, London, and which Éric Alliez has recently articulated from a Deleuzian and Guattarian angle in such texts as 'Rhizome (With no return)' (2011), further developed in his contribution to this issue.
2. 'La philosophie n'est ni contemplation, ni réflexion ni communication. Elle est l'activité qui crée les concepts. Comment se distingue-t-elle de ses rivales, qui prétendent nous fournir en concepts (comme le marketing aujourd'hui)? La philosophie doit nous dire quelle est la nature créative du concept, et quels en sont les concomitants: la pure immanence, le plan d'immanence, et les personnages conceptuels.
   Par là, la philosophie se distingue de la science et de la logique. Celles-ci n'opèrent pas par concepts, mais par fonctions, sur un plan de référence et avec des observateurs partiels. L'art opère par percepts et affects, sur un plan de composition avec des figures esthétiques. La philosophie n'est pas interdisciplinaire, elle est elle-même une discipline entière qui entre en résonance

avec la science et avec l'art, comme ceux-ci avec elle; trouver le concept d'une fonction, etc.

C'est que les trois plans sont les trois manières dont le cerveau recoupe le chaos, et l'affronte. Ce sont les chaoïdes. La pensée ne se constitue que dans ce rapport où elle risque toujours de sombrer' (Deleuze and Guattari [1991] 1994: back cover).

We owe special thanks to Marjorie Gracieuse for drawing our attention to this passage in her paper 'Immanence as Differential Material of Human Practices: on the distinction between Transdisciplinarity and Interdisciplinarity', presented at the conference.

3. This is the 'creative act' itself, which, as Deleuze puts it in his lecture from 1987, involves the construction of different modes of ideation:

'No one has an idea in general. An idea – like the one who has the idea – is already dedicated to a particular field. Sometimes it is an idea in painting, or an idea in an novel, or an idea in philosophy or an idea in science [...] Ideas have to be treated like potentials already *engaged* in one mode of expression or another' (Deleuze [2001] 2007: 317; original emphasis).

How can we visualise such a practice of thought? We may borrow here Jean-Claude Dumoncel's image: disciplines are paths of thought that travel in caravans, and Ideas are the 'caravanserais' where disciplines can enter from the various gateways and intersect 'independently of their specific technicalities' (Dumoncel 2009: 83; our translation):

'Les Idées, au sens deleuzien, sont donc des caravansérails de la pratique et de la pensée où peuvent se croiser les disciplines les plus diverses, indépendamment de leurs technicités spécifiques.'

References

Alliez, Éric (2011) 'Rhizome (With no return)', *Radical Philosophy*, 167 (May/Jun), pp. 36–42.

Badiou, Alain [1997] (2000) *Deleuze: The Clamour of Being*, trans. Louise Burchill, Minneapolis: University of Minnesota Press.

Deleuze, Gilles [1983] (1986) *Cinema 1: The Movement-Image*, trans. Hugh Tomlinson and Barbara Habberjam, London: Athlone Press.

Deleuze, Gilles [1985] (1989) *Cinema 2: The Time-Image*, trans. Hugh Tomlinson and Robert Galeta, London: Athlone Press.

Deleuze, Gilles [1968] (1994) *Difference and Repetition*, trans. Paul Patton, London: Athlone Press.

Deleuze, Gilles [1990] (1995) *Negotiations 1972–1990*, trans. Martin Joughin, New York: Columbia University Press.

Deleuze, Gilles [1995] (2001) *Pure Immanence. Essays on A Life*, trans. Anne Boyman, New York: Zone Books.

Deleuze, G. (2004) *Desert Islands and Other Texts: 1953–1974*, ed. D. Lapoujade, trans. M.Taormina, Los Angeles and New York: Semiotext(e).

Deleuze, Gilles [2001] (2007) *Two Regimes of Madness*, ed. David Lapoujade, trans. Ames Hodges and Mike Taormina, New York: Semiotext(e).

Deleuze, Gilles and Félix Guattari [1980] (1987) *A Thousand Plateaus: Capitalism and Schizophrenia*, trans. Brian Massumi, Minneapolis: University of Minnesota Press.

Deleuze, Gilles and Félix Guattari [1991] (1994) *What is Philosophy?*, trans. Hugh Tomlinson and Graham Burchill, London: Verso.

Dumoncel, Jean-Claude (2009) *Deleuze face à face*, Paris: M-editer.
Foucault, Michel [1984] (1985) *The Use of Pleasure, Volume 2 of The History of Sexuality*, trans. Robert Hurley, New York: Vintage.
Stengers, Isabelle (2005) 'Deleuze and Guattari's Last Enigmatic Message', *Angelaki*, 10:2, pp. 151–67.

Deleuze Challenges Kolmogorov on a Calculus of Problems

Jean-Claude Dumoncel   University of Caen

Abstract[1]

In 1932 Kolmogorov created a calculus of problems. This calculus became known to Deleuze through a 1945 paper by Paulette Destouches-Février. In it, he ultimately recognised a deepening of mathematical intuitionism. However, from the beginning, he proceeded to show its limits through a return to the Leibnizian project of *Calculemus* taken in its metaphysical stance. In the carrying out of this project, which is illustrated through a paradigm borrowed from Spinoza, the formal parallelism between problems, Leibnizian themes and Peircean rhemes provides the key idea. By relying on this parallelism and by spreading the dialectic defined by Lautman with its 'logical drama' onto a Platonic perspective, we will attempt to obtain Deleuze's full calculus of problems. In investigating how the same Idea may be in mathematics and in philosophy, we will proceed to show how this calculus of problems qualifies not only as a paradigm of the Idea but also as the apex of transdiciplinarity.[2]

Keywords: calculus, Deleuze, problems, rhemes, transcendentals,

I. Introduction

Transdisciplinarity has two conceptual neighbours or challengers in neighbourhood: pluridisciplinarity and interdisciplinarity. Pluridisciplinarity reaches its apex in anthropology: a man falling from a cliff is a point for mathematics, a body for physics, an organism for biology, perhaps a candidate for suicide for sociology. Interdisciplinarity, if it

Deleuze Studies 7.2 (2013): 169–193
DOI: 10.3366/dls.2013.0101
© Edinburgh University Press
www.euppublishing.com/dls

exists, is constantly in danger of falling prey to fashion. In a congress of mathematicians, physicists and epigraphists, the first condition of 'interdisciplinarity' is that mathematicians make mathematics, physicists physics and epigraphists epigraphy; but the second condition is that each also says something in the disciplines about which he or she is supposed to have a lot to learn. In this sense, 'interdisciplinarity' can be said to have as many advantages as squaring the circle does. And so the suspicion is born that mathematicians, physicists and epigraphists go to interdisciplinary jamborees in the rare periods when they really have nothing particular to say in mathematics, physics or epigraphy, respectively.

But what about this *tertium datur* between the Necessary and the Impossible that is transdisciplinarity? It is fairly easy to notice that the whole universe of pluridisciplinarity and interdisciplinarity turns in the circle of Comte's classification of the sciences: mathematics, physics, biology, sociology (and other social sciences). In other words, pluridisciplinarity and interdisciplinarity are by-products of positivism. Since universities, still bearing the vestiges of their medieval mothers, currently include a department of philosophy on a par with the faculties of theology, medicine and law, philosophers are also invited by force or politeness in the interdisciplinary jamborees. But the status of their discourse remains a mystery for all the participants, including themselves.

In the Deleuzian doctrine of Thought, however, we do have a concept for transdisciplinarity. This is the concept of the Idea, taken in the sense that the same Idea may be, for example, an Idea in mathematics, in cinema and in philosophy. In relation, then, to the positivist encyclopaedia, which circumscribes the whole territory of interdisciplinarity as well as pluridisciplinarity, we notice that Deleuze exceeds this Procrustean bed at least in two ways. First, philosophy acquires, in addition to its *de facto* status inherited from the medieval university, a *de jure* status reminiscent of its role in Plato's Academy or Aristotle's Lyceum. Second, the extension of Ideas is not confined to sciences (even *sensu lato*) but includes arts, such as cinema. Starting with this freed space of the Idea, we will focus on the couple philosophy–mathematics. With regard to this couple, the relation of Deleuze to Kolmogorov and the latter's calculus of problems offers more than a paradigm: rather, it opens a royal path, which, incidentally, also encounters the main difficulties surrounding what we will call the problem predicament.

Deleuze's assessment of the calculus of problems in symbolic logic is contained in two sentences that must be quoted in reverse chronological order:

> The 'intuitionist' school (Brouwer, Heyting, Griss, Bouligand, etc.) is of great importance in mathematics, not because it asserted the irreducible rights of intuition, or even because it elaborated a very novel constructivism, but because it developed a conception of *problems*, and of a *calculus of problems* that intrinsically rivals axiomatics and proceeds by other rules (notably with regard to the excluded middle). (Deleuze and Guattari [1980] 1987: 570)

> The calculus of problems as it is defined – notably by Kolmogoroff – still remains traced from a calculus of propositions, in 'isomorphism' with it. (Deleuze [1968] 1994: 322)[3]

The question faced in these two sentences is precisely indicative of the problem predicament. The first sentence contains the Deleuzian synopsis of mathematical intuitionism, which is better, as we shall see, than its counterparts in standard companions on the foundations of mathematics.[4] The second sentence is the Deleuzian challenge to Kolmogorov on the calculus of problems.[5] Yet there is a crucial connection between the two: the 'etc.' following the names of Brouwer and Heyting in the first sentence must be taken to refer primarily to Kolmogorov in the second. For, as it is well known, the calculus of problems, which according to Deleuze is the highpoint of mathematical intuitionism, had been created by Kolmogorov in 1932. This entails that the first sentence, which appears in *A Thousand Plateaus* in 1980, is an important correction of the position taken in 1968 in *Difference and Repetition*. In the latter, the calculus of Kolmogorov was simply seen as illustrating a 'false conception of the category of problem'; accordingly, its value was dismissed (Deleuze [1968] 1994: 322). In *A Thousand Plateaus*, however, the calculus of problems has reached the level of 'great mathematical importance'. As we shall see, this does not mean that the critical assessment is wholly withdrawn. In fact, the main reason behind Deleuze's enduring critical stance is his endorsement of the most celebrated among the Leibnizian 'dreams', that is, 'the great logical dream of a problem calculus'. For the *locus classicus* of this dream is the paragraph where Leibniz precisely anticipates the effect of his 'philosophical grammar' on Philosophy as a whole:

> Then, between two philosophers, there will be no more need of discussions longer than between mathematicians, since it will suffice that they seize their

pen, that they sit at their computing table (appealing to a friend if they wish) and that they say to each other: 'Let us calculate' [*Calculemus*]. (Leibniz [1687] 1978: 200)[6]

Regarding our question, then, in *Difference and Repetition*, Deleuze essentially draws on two tenets:[7] on the one hand, he endorses 'the great logical dream of a combinatory or calculus of problems' he ascribes to Leibniz (Deleuze [1968] 1994: 157);[8] on the other, he says about Carnot's *Reflections on the Metaphysics of the Infinitesimal Calculus* that '[by] invoking the notions of "problem" and "problem conditions" ... Carnot opened up for metaphysics a path which went beyond the frame of his own theory' (177). So that with regard to what we have called the problem predicament, the whole Deleuzian doctrine may be described as outlining a metaphysical calculus of problems. As we shall see, this view is maintained until *What Is Philosophy?* and it is precisely what subtends the definition of a properly Deleuzian dialectics. For according to Deleuze, 'Dialectic is the art of problems and questions, the combinatory or calculus of problems as such' (157). And in this dialectics, the metaphysical calculus of problems is the spearhead, and the theory of problems is more specifically called 'problematics'.[9]

Based on the above, our whole exposition will have two main, though unequal, parts. In the first part, which is relatively brief, we shall explain the Kolmogorov calculus and its discussion by Deleuze. In the second part, relying on scattered data in Deleuze, we shall disclose, through their systematisation, his full metaphysical calculus of problems.

II. The Kolmogorov Calculus of Problems

We have a double reason to expound upon and discuss the calculus of Kolmogorov. We must understand why Deleuze arrived at a positive assessment of it; and we must also find in it the target of his lasting critic on the problem predicament, explaining why the very same calculus falls short of the 'great logical dream'.

In order to appraise the Deleuzian judgement in its two pronouncements, we may condense the Kolmogorov calculus of problems in the four following definitions:

1. $A \wedge B$ is the problem of solving problem A *and* problem B.
2. $A \vee B$ is the problem of solving *at least* one of problems A *or* B.
3. $A \rightarrow B$ is the problem of reducing a solution of problem B to a solution of problem A (conditional problem).

4. ¬ *A* is the problem: assuming a solution of problem *A* exists, deduce a contradiction.

Based on the logic so defined, we shall try to answer two questions: first, what is the 'great importance in mathematics' of this calculus 'notably with regard to the excluded middle'? Second, why does it nonetheless miss, according to Deleuze, the true 'conception of the category of problem'?

According to the standard story, as concerns the calculus of problems Kolmogorov is credited with having provided the 'semantics' of intuitionist logic. This is not false, but when Deleuze asserts that the calculus of problems 'intrinsically rivals axiomatics and proceeds by other rules (notably with regard to the excluded middle)' (Deleuze and Guattari [1980] 1987: 570), he is pointing to a much more important performance. As we shall see, the main contribution of Kolmogorov to intuitionist logic is a real foundation of this deviant logic in his calculus of problems. Taken in this perspective, 'intuitionist' logic is better called 'constructive' logic.

In order to see this point more clearly, it should suffice to deepen the comparison between two of the best-known laws in formal logic, here presented in a Kolmogorov dress. We mean the *tertium non datur* (or principle of 'the excluded middle')

$$A \vee \neg A$$

and the *modus ponens*

$$(A \wedge (A \rightarrow B)) \rightarrow B.$$

Between these two laws, the universal validity of the *tertium non datur* was notoriously questioned by Brouwer; and the first contribution of Kolmogorov to intuitionist logic is in his 1925 paper 'On the Principle of Excluded Middle'. Indeed, in the seemingly homogeneous web of the propositional calculus where these laws are selected, the Kolmogorov calculus of problems will reveal an unsuspected break.

Suppose the problem A ∧ (A → B) has a solution. This means that we have a solution to problem A and a solution to problem A → B. But a solution of problem A → B means that the solution of problem B may be reduced to a solution of problem A. And, by hypothesis, we have a solution of problem A. So we have also a solution of problem B. All this means that the solution of problem B may be reduced to a solution of problem A ∧ (A → B) – that is, the exact case of (A ∧ (A → B)) → B. In other words, the *modus ponens* works in the calculus of problems exactly like it does in the standard propositional calculus. But with the *tertium non datur*, it is a different ball game! Because here we hit at the difference between

$$A \vee \neg A$$

and the crude

$$p \vee \neg p.$$

The classical $p \vee \neg p$, for its part, means only that in any couple $\langle p, \neg p \rangle$ of contradictory propositions one at least is true. But with $A \vee \neg A$, it is quite another story because in this case we have either a solution of problem A or a solution of problem $\neg A$. And having a solution to any problem is an epistemic endorsement. Thus, the *tertium non datur* which, in a calculus of truth functions is a valid law, reveals itself to be subject to an 'impeachment' when the calculus of problems enters the landscape.[10]

Let us illustrate the above point with a celebrated example revisited by Deleuze: 'Will there be a naval battle tomorrow?' (Deleuze [1985] 1989: 130). This is a problem. As Aristotle says, 'it is necessary that there will be a sea-battle tomorrow or not' (Aristotle, qtd in Anscombe 1956).[11] This gives us an illustration of $p \vee \neg p$. But $A \vee \neg A$ is the problem of solving *at least* one of problems A or $\neg A$, where $\neg A$ is the problem: assuming a solution of problem A exists, deduce a contradiction. So that in this case $A \vee \neg A$ is the problem of having either a demonstrably true prognostic of a sea-battle tomorrow or a *reductio ad absurdum* of such a prognostic. We sublunar mortals are far off this epistemic performance. In other words, we may say that in the practice of problems, the transmission of obtained solutions along the channel of implication can conduce to the detachment of a solution according to the step of the *modus ponens*, but that on the fork of a disjunction there is no adjudication of solutions isomorphic to a *tertium non datur* (this alternative adjudication being confined to the truth values).

The difference between the respective destinies of the *modus ponens* and the *tertium non datur*, when the calculus of problems makes the difference, is of a huge significance. It means that formal logic, on the level of the propositional calculus, is crossed by an essential heterogeneity. The *modus ponens* is paradigmatic of the logical principles as laws of thought. With the *tertium non datur* we are on another territory. As the sea-battle predicament shows, the *tertium non datur* is a law of being and becoming. The calculus of problems reveals the objective difference between the two kinds of laws by epistemological criteria. And when the epistemological considerations are predominant, as in mathematical intuitionism, the verdict of the epistemological criteria is promoted to the status of a logical touchstone: so much so that the principle of excluded middle is rejected as a logical rule.

In all this, as it will be obvious by now, the isomorphism duly registered by Deleuze has an essential function: it is because the symbolic formulas of the calculus of problems, literally taken, are indiscernible from the corresponding formulas in the propositional calculus that the calculus of problems has a discriminating power on the propositional calculus. In other words, the calculus of problems detects differences in the propositional calculus on condition that it is (morphologically) identical to it. 'Difference' is detected by (literal) 'repetition'. But on the level of the whole predicament, this means that the Kolmogorov calculus is a kind of medal, with its reverse and its obverse. For in the Deleuzian balance, the same isomorphism that motivates the critical attitude on the calculus is also a key condition of the discriminating power which constitutes its value. Nevertheless, there is no inconsistency between the two faces of the medal. On the contrary, the more the Deleuzian assessment recognises the unquestionable value of the Kolmogorov breakthrough, the more its reservations are well anchored, with its own doctrine well erected.

III. The Metaphysical Calculus of Problems

It must be noted that Kolmogorov does not define the notion of 'problem' but gives only some examples. These are the paradigmatic problems according to Kolmogorov. One of these examples is the following:

Find four positive integers x, y, z, n, such that $x^n + y^n = z^n$ and $n > 2$.

Here we can already recognise the target of the Fermat–Wiles theorem. A truly tiny target for a truly titanic proof! But this paradigmatic problem of mathematics leads us to an exegetic problem in philosophy: where in Deleuze do we find an example on the level of Kolmogorov's?

To our knowledge, taking into account that the Deleuzian concept of a calculus derives in part from the 'metaphysics of the calculus' in Carnot and that the paradigmatic problem of Kolmogorov is a case of exponentiation, this is an *apax*:[12]

> Hegel shows that variability in the function is not confined to values that can be changed (2/3 and 4/6), or are left indetermined ($a = 2b$), but requires one of the variables to be at a higher power ($y^2/x = P$). For it is then that a relation can be directly determined as differential relation dy/dx, in which

the only determination of the value of the variables is that of disappearing or being born, even though it is wrested from infinite speeds. A state of affairs or 'derivative' function depends on such a relation: an operation of depotentialisation has been carried out that makes possible the comparison of distinct powers starting from which a thing or a body may well develop (integration). (Deleuze and Guattari [1991] 1994: 122)

These lines from *What Is Philosophy?* are directly referred to a page by Hegel in the *Science of Logic* [1816] (2010).[13] In fact, they are an abstract of two or three pages of Hegel's on the differential and integral calculus – a strange abstract, no less, because it admits of a double reading.[14] Upon a first reading, it can be said to follow some lines on the representation of velocity and acceleration in the famous diagram of Nicole Oresme, so that we have in two pages a philosophical epitome of the infinitesimal calculus considered in its genesis and evolution, a subject which Deleuze had studied at length in *The History of the Calculus and its Conceptual Development* by Carl B. Boyer.[15] A second reading is induced by a tiny anomaly of the text. In his abstract of Hegel on the calculus, Deleuze retains the examples given in the *Science of Logic* but with one exception. Hegel begins his series of examples by the equality $2/7 = 4/14$. Without any warning, Deleuze replaces it by the equality $2/3 = 4/6$. Why? We are in a book where Spinoza is proclaimed 'the prince of philosophers' (Deleuze and Guattari [1991] 1994: 48). So we can recognise here 'the proportion 2, 4, 3, 6', taken as example from the *Treatise on the Emendation of the Intellect.*[16] And this proportion illustrates a general request: 'Three numbers are given – it is required to find a fourth, which shall be to the third as the second is to the first.' That is, we are here before a paradigm of the problem. In the *Ethics* (II, XL, n. 2), this paradigm is even made both more simple and more explicit: 'one, two, three, being given, everyone can see that the fourth proportional is six'. In this version, the paradigm is more simple since it begins with the three first numbers; and it is more explicit as a case of problem since only the given numbers 1, 2 and 3 are named, leaving the solution of the problem in the dark or, better, as a blank. So, if we put this paradigm in the same form as $2/3 = 4/6$, we obtain

$$1/2 = 3/\ .$$

This is the Deleuzian paradigm of problem. And now that we have this paradigm, we may proceed to its dogmatic exposition. It has the nice form of an ABC.

Problems, Rhemes and Themes in the Procession of a Same Theme

We are also in a chapter of *What Is Philosophy?* where the first sentence declares: 'The objects of science are not concepts, but functions ...'. The sequel of this thesis is to be found in the first page of the following chapter, where Deleuze, speaking about logic, says that 'following the route marked out by Frege and Russell, it wants to turn the concept into a function' (Deleuze and Guattari [1991] 1994: 135). Deleuze adds the condition of this transgression: 'Thus a new, specifically logical type of function must be invented', the 'propositional function'. And he gives an example of propositional function:

x is human.

But this is only the parvis of the temple. Because Deleuze knows as well the paradigm of the giving in C. S. Peirce (Deleuze [1983] 1986: 197). He writes it as:

A 'gives' B to C.

In Peirce we find the following writing:

−**gives** ¬ **to** −   (Peirce [1898] 1992: 154)

And Deleuze has adopted this writing by hyphens on the case of the Other as a paradigm of concept with two components: 'its concept is that of an other–a subject that presents itself as an object–which is special in relation to the self' (Deleuze and Guattari [1991] 1994: 16). Peirce explains this kind of writing in the definition of his concept of rheme, also written 'rhema':

> If parts of a proposition be erased so as to leave blanks in their place, and if these blanks are of such a nature that if each of them be filled by a proper name the result will be a proposition, then the blank form of proposition which was first produced by the erasures is termed a rheme. According as the number of blanks in a rheme is 0, 1, 2, 3, etc., it may be termed a *medad* (from $\mu\eta\delta$, nothing), *monad*, *dyad*, *triad*, etc., rheme. (Peirce [1903] 1998: 299)

> In a complete proposition there are no blanks. It may be called a *medad*, or *medadic relative*, from $\mu\eta\delta\alpha\mu\delta\varsigma$, none, and $-\dot{\alpha}\delta\alpha$, the accusative ending of such words $\mu ov\dot{\alpha}\varsigma$, $\delta v\dot{\alpha}\varsigma$, $\tau\rho\iota\dot{\alpha}\varsigma$, $\tau\varepsilon\tau\rho\dot{\alpha}\varsigma$ etc. A non-relative name with a substantive verb, as '– is a man', or 'man that is –', or '–'s manhood' has one blank; it is a *monad*, or *monadic relative*. An ordinary relative with an active verb as '– is a lover of –' or 'the loving by – of –' has two blanks; it is a *dyad*, or *dyadic* relative. A higher relative similarly treated has a plurality of blanks. It may be called a *polyad*. The rank of a relative among these may be called its

adinity, that is the peculiar quality of the number it embodies. (Peirce 1933: CP 3.465, 294)

But all this means that the rheme of Peirce is exactly the same thing as the propositional function of Russell as a case of the function of Frege. 'A gives B to C' is only a notational variant of 'x gives y to z'. And since the Deleuzian writing of the concept is borrowed from the Peircean writing of the rheme, the conclusion seems unavoidable: Deleuze himself has remelted the concept of Concept in the mould of the function. What Peirce has labelled 'adinity', now called 'arity' by the logician, is in the vocabulary of Deleuze a case of *multiplicity* (Deleuze and Guattari [1991] 1994: 15).

We must, however, remark that this reasoning does not go without saying for the Peircean step:

$$- \text{ gives } \neg \text{ to } -$$

As we may notice, in the Peircean paradigm of the giving, we have to distinguish three heterogeneous 'roles': the donor A, the donee C, and the gift B. And the juridical difference between the persons and the things is appropriately marked by a difference between the allotted hyphens '$-$' and '$\neg$ '. This implies that here the limits of formal logic are exceeded, since the difference donor/donee, for example, pertains to the matter of the meaning. And such a difference of roles defines, as we shall see, a stepping stone for the Deleuzian logic of problems.

The key concept, here, is exhumed by Deleuze when, in opposition to the Kolmogorov calculus, he takes up[17] a notion that Leibniz himself had borrowed from 'some logicians of the reformation century': the concept of theme which immediately divides itself in incomplex theme and complex theme according to the distinction between 'ideas or terms' and 'propositions or truths' (Leibniz 1992: IV, i, § 2).

In these Leibnizian terms, an incomplex theme is 'a thing or idea', such as 'in love', and a complex theme is 'a thesis, proposition or truth' such as 'Candide is in love' or 'Candide is in love with Cunegonde'. As it is well known, from a propositional function such as 'x has a daemon', propositions are obtained by what Frege has described as the saturation of the function, that is, either by the substitution of constants for the variables – as in 'Socrates has a daemon' – or by quantifying on the variables – as in '$\exists x.\ x$ has a daemon' ('There is an x such that x has a daemon'). This means that the conceptual couple incomplex theme/complex theme is the ancestor of the conceptual couple propositional function/proposition (x is in love/everybody is in love, etc.).

But Deleuze quotes the following lines from Leibniz:

> There are indeed 'themes' which can be said to be midway between an idea and a proposition, namely *questions*. Some of these ask for the Yes or the No, and these are the closest to propositions; but there are others which ask the how and the circumstances, and so on, and more must be added to these if they are to become propositions. (Leibniz 1981: IV, i, § 2)

For example, we have the following procession on a same theme:

[a] — is in love

[b] Is Marcel in love?

[c] Marcel is in love with Albertine.

In this paradigm, [a] is a term, [b] is a question (formulation of a possible problem) and [c] is a proposition. But the procession [a]–[b]–[c] as a whole is on a same theme. From the Deleuzian point of view, this is the fundamental fact of logic. And in the conceptual conflict with Kolmogorov, this is exactly what challenges the isomorphism so well exploited by Kolmogorov, for example between '$p \wedge q$' and '$A \wedge B$'. As its name recalls, iso*morph*ism is identity of form. The thematic identity, on the contrary, is an identity of matter, content or topic. It is an 'iso*hyl*ism' or, better, iso*top*ism.

Let us compare the formulas of the following thematic table:

(1) $1/2 = 3/x$	[1] Pleasure/$x = y/z$
(2) $1/2 = 3/6$	[2] Pleasure/Act $=$ Beauty/Youth in its flower
(3) $x/2 = 3/6$	[3] x/ Act $=$ Beauty/Youth in its flower
(4) $x/y = 3/6$	[4] x/ y = Beauty/Youth in its flower
(5) $x/y = z/6$	[5] $x/y = z$/Youth in its flower
(6) $x/y = z/w$	[6] $x/y = z/w$
(7) $2/y = z/w$	[7] Queen/$y = z/w$
(8) $2/4 = z/w$	[8] Queen/Monarchy $= z/w$
(9) $2/4 = 5/w$	[9] Queen/Monarchy $=$ President/w
(10) $2/4 = 5/10$	[10] Queen/Monarchy $=$ President/Republic

In this table, we must begin with line 6, where (6) = [6], being a propositional function with four free variables. From this starting point, we can then proceed either downwards or upwards. If we proceed downwards, along the series from (5) to (10) or [5] to [10], following the method recalled by Deleuze when he says that we arrive at '*f*(*a*) for a variable *x*', we shall obtain finally, by the progressive elimination of all the free variables, a proposition that is true or false such as (10) or [10]: '2/4 equals 5/10' or 'The queen is to a monarchy what the president is to a republic'. This is the logical genesis of propositions by quantification binding the free variables of the propositional function or by substitution of constants for these variables. Here, it is illustrated by the second method, the more fundamental one.

But if we proceed upwards, we penetrate into another territory. First, we must notice that a formula such as (1)

$$1/2 = 3/x$$

is virtually ambiguous. If it is taken in a book of formal logic, it is probably, as (9), a propositional function with one free variable, on a par with the Deleuzian example '*x* is human'. If it is taken in a book of mathematics, it is probably a proposition. This proposition may be formulated, as in Kolmogorov, under the form of an imperative:

Find one integer *x* such that $1/2 = 3/x$.

But it may also take the form of an interrogative proposition:

What is the number *x* such that $1/2 = 3/x$?

In its two forms, the proposition enunciates a problem by an equation. In a propositional function the variables are dummies disposed of in order to be clothed by constants. In an equation they are the unknown variables, here to be suppressed by their solutions. (By 'virtually ambiguous', we mean that the ambiguity cannot cause any misunderstanding since propositional functions with free variables have no use – but only mentions. Consequently, the amphibology is recommended as an economy!)

The case of '$1/2 = 3/x$' may be generalised. When in our table we proceed from (6) to (3) and (1) or from [6] to [3] and [1], we obtain in each column some examples of (soluble or insoluble) problems. The propositions (2) and [2] contain respectively the solutions of problems (1) and [1]. Therefore, we arrive at the following conclusion: the arity or adinity of propositional functions extends to the problems, taking the form of the number of their unknown variables. In Deleuzian terms, this means that the multiplicity characteristic of the rhemes extends to the problems or, better, that the same multiplicity extends indifferently to propositional functions and to problems. Since problems are naturally expressed in questions and since the logic of questions is called erotetic logic (from the Greek *erotesis*, questioning) we shall call this thesis of a same arity shared by all themes (in rhemes and problems) the principle of rhema-erotetic arity.

This thesis must be appreciated in its full significance. Formal logic, in its totality, is constituted by the propositional calculus and quantification theory. But since propositions are nothing but saturated propositional functions and since quantification is the binding of variables in propositional functions, the concept of propositional function is the arch-concept of logic in its totality. The fact that the arity of propositional functions exceeds formal logic and qualifies also the problems, therefore, may be said the fundamental fact of logic.

In taking from Spinoza the $1/2 = 3/x$ as paradigm of problems, endorsing the hyphen symbolism of Peircean rhemes and recycling the Leibnizian themes, Deleuze has discovered on the path problem–rheme–theme the principle of rhema-erotetic arity as the thesis of isotopy.

In Kolmogorov's calculus, the only problems at stake are mathematical problems. But, as the thematic table shows, the principle of isotopy is not confined to mathematics. As the example from Aristotle attests, philosophical problems illustrate the same law. The problem [1] may be rephrased more explicitly:

[1bis] Found a good analogy exhibiting the place of pleasure in human life.

In order to reach the full generality of a calculus of problems, how can we neutralise the difference between philosophy and mathematics? Following Coquand in his commentary on Kolmogorov,[18] we shall introduce the conceptual character imagined by Hilbert: **Aristide** $= \tau_x A$. The so-called Aristide is defined by Hilbert in the following way: if A is the predicate 'to be corruptible', then $\tau_x A$ would be a man 'of such absolute integrity that, if he happened to be corruptible, all men in general would be corruptible' (Hilbert [1923] 1996: 1140–1; translation modified). With such a definition, Hilbert's Aristide is obviously an amphibian between mathematics and philosophy.

But in order to reach such a result, and even if, as Kolmogorov, one confines the calculus to mathematics, the fundamental fact of logic itself is not sufficient. Deleuze declares:

> Sense is located in the problem itself. Sense is constituted in the complex theme, but the complex theme is that set of problems and questions in relation to which the propositions serve as elements of response and cases of solution. (Deleuze [1968] 1994: 157)

This thesis precedes the reference to Leibniz[19] which leads us to his division of the concept of theme into complex themes and incomplex themes. As we have seen, in Leibniz, an incomplex theme is for example 'in love' or 'in love with Cunegonde', and a complex theme is, for example, 'Candide is in love' or 'Candide is in love with Cunegonde'. That is, in Leibniz, incomplex themes are terms to be conceived as rhemes or propositional functions, and complex themes are propositions. But when we penetrate into the Deleuzian dialectics, the opposition incomplex/complex acquires an entirely new meaning.

In order to understand the Deleuzian dialectics in its full significance, we have to enlarge our conceptual apparatus and consider at least the following conceptual triplet that we shall call the entire dialectic triad:

$$\text{Problems}$$
$$\text{Terms} = \text{Rhemes} = \text{Propositional functions}$$
$$\text{Propositions}$$

In the dialectic triad, the layer of rhemes represents the level of incomplex themes. But the main point of Deleuzian dialectics is that, from this layer of incomplexity, two kinds of logical 'complexity' can be reached; two kinds that are not only different but entirely heterogeneous.

There is the well-known complexity of propositions, which qualifies them as complex themes in the Leibnizian sense. This is the 'complexity' obtained by the saturation of rhemes as propositional functions. For example, from the incomplex

$$x/y = z/w$$

there is the increasing complexity of

$$x/y = z/\text{Aristide}$$
$$\exists x.x/y = z/\text{Aristide}$$
$$\text{Etc.}$$

But there is a quite different complexity in the bargain: the complexity qualifying the problems.

Lautman in Bergsonian territory: incipit Albert Lautman

From here onwards, the Deleuzian doctrine on problems is mainly borrowed from Lautman.[20] In mathematical philosophy, the Lautman posture is an *apax*. On the category of problem, according to Deleuze, Lautman is grasped in a kind of analogy with the doctrine of Bergson on intuition, intelligence and instinct. According to Bergson, between intelligence and instinct we find the following chiasmatic paradox:

Intelligence sets problems of which it has no solution.
Instinct has solutions of problems it has never set.

The function of intuition follows:

Intuition has the function of giving to the problems of intelligence the ready-made solutions worked out by instinct.

Mathematics is, among others, a case of this Law of Bergson. In mathematics, as in other disciplines, the solutions are the affair of an 'instinct'. And the royal art is the weaving of unforeseeable problems by intelligence. This is the true story of mathematical 'intuition'.

This paradoxical situation is paralleled by the main relation between philosophy and mathematics as it is conceived by Lautman. According to Lautman, philosophy sets latent problems to which it has no solution, and mathematics offers patent solutions of some problems it has never set. The task of 'mathematical philosophy' follows: mathematical philosophy must give to the latent problems of philosophy their patent solutions in mathematics:

> Nowhere better than in the admirable work of Albert Lautman has it been shown how problems are first Platonic Ideas or ideal liaisons between *dialectical* notions, relative to 'eventual situations of the existent'; but also how they are realised within the real relations constitutive of the desired solution within a *mathematical, physical* or other field. It is in this sense, according to Lautman, that science always participates in a dialectic which points beyond it – in other words, in a meta-mathematical and extra-propositional power – even though the liaisons of this dialectic are incarnated only in effective scientific propositions and theories. (Deleuze [1968] 1994: 163–4)

The mathematical philosophy of Lautman, itself, is exfoliated on two Platonic plateaus: on a first plateau, Lautman holds that even 'at the mathematical level' there is a real 'drama' which is 'played' in the heights, and that it qualifies as a 'logical drama' (Lautman [2006] 2011: 167, 189). On a second plateau, this logical drama, played at the level of mathematics, is in its turn explained by an even more secret history or action, developing itself 'at the background' of the drama, or, more exactly, above it. This double doctrine is contained in the following lines:

> Mathematics, and above all modern mathematics, algebra, group theory and topology, have thus appeared to us to tell, in addition to the constructions in which the mathematician is interested, another more hidden story made for

the philosopher. A dialectical action is always at play in the background ...
(Lautman [2006] 2011: 91)

One may say that distinct mathematical theories participate to a common
dialectic which dominates them ... participation of mathematics to a higher
and more hidden reality which, in my opinion, constitute a real world of
ideas. (Lautman, qtd in Cavaillès [1939] 1946: 596, 605; also Cavaillès 1994:
596, 605; my translation)

This action, which is played above the Lautmanian drama, will be
called the Lautmanian *gesta*. Corresponding to these two plateaux of
Lautman's theory, Deleuzian dialectics will itself develop in a drama
crowned by a *gesta*.

The proper complexity of problems, taken in its main lines, is
described by Deleuze as follows: 'The complete determination of
a problem is inseparable from the existence, the number and the
distribution of the determinant points *which precisely provide its
conditions* (one singular point gives rise to two condition equations)'
(Deleuze [1968] 1994: 163; [1969] 1990: 54).[21] Here we have an
ascending dialectic of four floors:

> 4th The singular determinant points giving rise to the equations.
> 3rd The equations of conditions.
> 2nd The conditions of the problem.
> 1st The problem.

In this ascending dialectics, the conditions of a problem and the equation
of conditions are borrowed by Deleuze from Carnot (Deleuze [1968]
1994: 175):

after having introduced these quantities in the calculus in order to facilitate
the expression of the conditions of the problem, and having treated them, in
the equations which expressed these conditions, as zero by comparison with
the proposed quantities, in order to simplify these equations, it suffices to
eliminate these same quantities ... (Carnot [1881] 1970: 11)

The 'conditions of a problem' are a case of dialectical amphibian.
Suppose that the problem is

$$x = 100 - a.$$

Here, a 'condition of the problem' is that $a \leq 100$, *if* we are confined to
natural numbers. But if we have at our disposal the algebraic numbers,
positive or negative, the 'condition' evaporates. And you know that
the same tale may be told for the invention of $\sqrt{2}$, 0, $\sqrt{-1}$, etc. In
other words, the whole history of mathematics may be rewritten as

the history of superstitious 'conditions' and their successive dissolutions in the ocean of heroic generalisation. But this positively means that, since the quadrature of the circle, the problems are the erotetic fountain from which the whole stream of mathematics flows with 'the rule and the compass' as paradigm of obsolete 'conditions' for a construction problem.

At the other extreme of the dialectical spectrum, the same 'conditions of a problem' are a matter of algebraic routine in the standard cooking of equations. Here, the paradigm is an interdict in mosaic form: 'Never divide by zero' ('Par zéro jamais ne diviseras!'). If this condition is not fulfilled, this is the problem ('set in equation') which evaporates. But in a descending dialectic, Deleuze relies first on a paradigm borrowed from Lautman, with two illustrations of the determinant points:

> [a] The cases that we are going to envisage[22] are those of the functions admitting 3 singular points: the points 0, 1 and ∞. It can still in effect be obtained by a linear transformation that the singularities are produced at these points here. (Lautman [2006] 2011: 179)

> [b] The points of indetermination[23] where $P = Q = 0$, constitute the singularities of the vector field. (Lautman [2006] 2011: 259)

The main fact here is that the two illustrations lead to the same conclusion on the singular points:

> [a*] the nature of singular points on a domain determines, at each point of the domain of the variable z, the existence of solutions of the proposed equation. (Lautman [2006] 2011: 181)

> [b*] The existence and distribution of singularities are notions relative to the vector field defined by the differential equations. The form of the integral curves is relative to the solutions of this equation. (Lautman [2006] 2011: 259)

So Deleuze can conclude:

> Albert Lautman has clearly indicated this difference in kind between the existence and distribution of singular points which refer to the problem-element, and the specification of these same points which refer to the solution-element. (Deleuze [1968] 1994: 324)

> For example, in the theory of differential equations, the existence and distribution of singularities are relative to a problematic field defined by the equation as such. As for the solution, it appears only with the integral curves and the form they take in the vicinity of singularities inside the field of vectors. (Deleuze [1969] 1990: 54)

As for the 'equations of conditions',[24] when the problem is in the differential equation

$$w'' + p_1(z)\, w' + p_2(z)\, w = 0$$

the two alluded 'equations of conditions'[25] are, at the vicinity of the point $z = a$ on the complex plane **C**:

$$w_1 = (z - a)_1^l\, P(z - a)$$

and

$$w_2 = (z - a)_2^l\, P^*(z - a) + \text{eventually a logarithmic term.}$$

But where is there a 'drama'? This term 'drama', used by Lautman, finds its best ratio in Proclus: 'Proclus defines the problem by means of the events which come to affect a logical subject matter (sections, ablations, adjunctions, etc.)' (Deleuze [1969] 1990: 54). In proper Proclean terms:[26] 'it is in imagination that the constructions, sectionings, superpositions, comparisons, additions and subtractions take place ...' (Proclus 1970: 64 [78]). But here, the problems whose complexity is exhibited by Lautman are typically equations. This means that we remain in the domain of mathematics. So, we do not see so far how this description could be valid about philosophical problems. In order, then, to reach the level on which the Deleuzian dialectics embraces as well philosophical and mathematical problems, we must move, in its Lautmanian top, from drama to *gesta*.

The Lautmanian Gesta and its Themes

Over and above the Lautmanian dialectical drama, what is the Lautmanian dialectical *gesta* of problems? The kind of themes providing the plots of this *gesta* are described by Lautman in the following terms:

> the materials of which the universe is formed are not so much the atoms and molecules of the physical theory as these great pairs of ideal opposites such as the Same and the Other, the Symmetrical and Dissymmetrical, related to one another according to the laws of a harmonious mixture. (Lautman [2006] 2011: xxviii)

This thesis must be labelled the Lautman Law. The 'great couples of ideal contraries' alluded in the Lautman Law have a celebrated register in a Pythagorean table:

1. Limit & Unlimited
2. Odd & Even

3. One & Many
4. Right & Left
5. Male & Female
6. Rest & Move
7. Straight & Curve
8. Light & Darkness
9. Good & Bad
10. Square & Oblong

Lautman simply adds to this table two homogeneous lines:

11. Same & Other
12. Symmetric & Dissymmetric

Here we understand why the theory of problems which dominates mathematics according to Plato and Lautman is called a dialectic by them. It is a dialectic because it is a doctrine of dualities. But in order to obtain in this dialectic a calculus of problems at the level envisioned by Leibniz, that is a calculus covering not only of mathematical but also of philosophical problems, the 'great couples of ideal contraries' alluded to by Lautman must extend to the whole register that is due to Plato. This list is drawn up in a dialogue between Socrates and Theaetetus:

> Soc. To which class, then, do you assign being; for this, more than anything else, belongs to all things? Theaet. I assign them to the class of notions which the soul grasps by itself directly. Soc. And also same and other [likeness and unlikeness] and identity and difference? Theaet. Yes. Soc. And how about beautiful and ugly, and good and bad? Theaet. I think that these also are among the things the essence of which the soul most certainly views in their relations to one another, reflecting within itself upon the past and present in relation to the future. (Plato 1921: 186ab)

With this ultimate adjunction:

> Soc. Is it possible for one to attain 'truth' who cannot even get as far as being? Theaet. No. (Plato 1921: 186c, pp. 163–5; translation modified)

This is in advance an inventory of the transcendental terms, enumerating the objects of philosophy. So, with these 'great couples of ideal contraries' enlisted in their complete enumeration, Lautmanian dialectics reaches its top level and the calculus of problems can satisfy the requisites of the Leibnizian programme. Because, from Plato's listing of transcendental terms to a calculus, there is only one step. This can be shown if we realise that Hilbert's Aristide is a kind of Platonic or Lautmanian 'Idea'. Aristide, as we may recall, is 'of such absolute integrity that, if he happened to be corruptible, all men in general would be corruptible' (Hilbert [1923] 1996: 1140–1; translation modified). Similarly, according to Plato, the Idea of the Good is of such absolute goodness that, if it happened to be bad, all things in general would be bad. Hilbert's Aristide, therefore, is only a personalisation of the Platonic Idea. So, along with Aristotelian or Stoic logic, with its Boolean and Fregean offspring, Hilbert has forged a Platonic logic. And Lautman, with his dialectics, has maximised the efficiency of Hilbert's Aristide.

Consequently, reconsider our paradigm of an amphibian problem:

$$x/y = z/\text{Aristide}.$$

According to Plato's analogy of the line, this paradigm must be vertically restated.[27] In this new manner it takes the following form:

Aristide

- - - - - - - - - -

z

$=$

y

- - - -

x

And on this ladder, at its top rung, since Aristide is only a personification of the Platonic Idea, he can be replaced by any analogous term, with its two main species, mathematical and philosophical. In the mathematical realm, a paradigm is already offered by Plato:

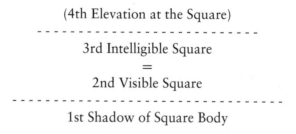

(4th Elevation at the Square)

- -

3rd Intelligible Square

$=$

2nd Visible Square

- -

1st Shadow of Square Body

Here, in mathematics, we follow an ascending dialectics: the stages x, y and z are given, and the problem is to find the 'fourth proportional' $= Power2 = (\ )^2$. In the philosophical realm, this is the other way round: in the whole vertical procession, Aristide is given at the top level, and the xyz series follows by measured participation to the Idea, in a triad of hypostases. For example, if Aristide = the Other:

$$\text{Other}$$
$$- - - - - - - - - - -$$
$$x$$
$$=$$
$$y$$
$$- - - -$$
$$z$$

So that, in its Lautmanian empyrean, the calculus of problems permits the deduction of the Platonic dialectics with its two inverse moves of ascending and descending dialectics. Accordingly, the metaphysical calculus of problems in its full development may be exposed in the following Lautmanian table:

	Lautman	Spinoza	Hilbert in Plato	Deleuze
Invisible	*Dialectics*	*x*	Aristide	**Same and Other**
Invisible	Mathematics	3	*a*	*Mathematics*
Visible	Natural philosophy	2	*b*	*Natural philosophy*
Visible	Physics	1	*c*	*Physics*

In this table, the essential fact to be read and emphasised is the difference between the three first columns and the fourth. In the Lautman column, physics, natural philosophy, and mathematics are *given*; the problem, situated at the level of dialectics, is the determination, as 'fourth proportional', of the 'X' which qualifies as the object of dialectics. In the Spinoza column, the *x* is the algebraic unknown variable to be found. In the Hilbert and Plato column, Aristide himself, after all, is only a dummy for Göttingen geometers. But in the Deleuzian column, all this indetermination is suppressed. With the Same and the Other (or similar transcendental terms), the Lautmanian dialectics receives its adequate Object, qualifying it as a philosophical calculus (philosophical, since Aristide becomes a transcendental term; and calculus since the entire column retains the algebraic form of its Spinoza counterpart). And all this means that the entire table functions as a mathematical proportion, where the fourth column is the solution, obtained as 'fourth proportional': QED.

IV. Conclusion

On the problem predicament, the Kolmogorov calculus of problems was received by Deleuze as the summit of mathematical intuitionism and as a challenge to the Leibnizian *Calculemus* in philosophy. The challenge is taken up at least in two results:

1. The thesis of isotopy disclosing the procession of a same theme in the Peircean rhemes and the Leibnizian problems.
2. The deduction of a Lautmanian dialectics where the Hilbertian Aristide is the variable whose values are the transcendental terms defining the objects of philosophy.

On the level of transdisciplinarity *qua* transdisciplinarity, this double result has a huge significance. Since the objects of philosophy are the transcendental terms (*esse, unum, verum, bonum* and *pulchrum*), philosophy transcends all categories, which are the top of all *generality*. And since the territory of all theoretical sciences is generality, philosophy transcends the whole territory of theoretical science. So, philosophy is 'transdisciplinary' by itself. But in the territory of science, mathematics is the top of apodicticity. Hence the Leibnizian programme of the *Calculemus*: to transport into philosophy the apodicticity of mathematics. In solving the proportional problem exposed in the Lautmanian table, Deleuze has accomplished the decisive step in this transfer.

Notes

1. Special acknowledgements are due to Marjorie Gracieuse, Chryssa Sdrolia and Masa Kosugi for their kind invitation to the Deleuzian symposium where this talk took place, for their generous and invaluable help, as well as for the logistics of our agapistic meeting and the sophisticated predicaments and intellectual delicacies, which make its growing attractiveness and spell.
2. Chryssa Sdrolia saw immediately that the oral version of my paper was better than the original written version. The following text is revised according to this trusty verdict.
3. In this paper, we will follow the alternate spelling 'Kolmogorov'.
4. With the exception of Carl Posy (2005) 'Intuitionism and Philosophy', in Stewart Shapiro (ed.), *The Oxford Handbook of Philosophy of Mathematics and Logic*, Oxford: Oxford University Press, but for very different reasons.
5. When Deleuze wrote that sentence, the unique source he referred to on the calculus of Kolmogorov was a Note by Paulette Destouches-Février to the French Academy of Sciences, 'Rapports entre le calcul des problèmes et le calcul des propositions', published in 1945.
6. 'Quo facto, quando orientur controversiae, non magis disputatione opus erit inter duos philosophos, quam inter duos Computistas. Sufficiet enim calamos

in manus sumere sedereque ad abacos, et sibi mutuo (accito si placet amico) dicere: Calculemus' (Leibniz [1687] 1978 '*Scientia Generalis, Characteristica*'; my translation).

7. From a genetic point of view, we must recall that *Difference and Repetition* was in Deleuze's PhD the 'thèse principale' and that its initial subject was the 'idea of problem' (Dosse [2007] 2010: 116–17).
8. *Différence & Répétition*, p. 204; (translation slightly modified).
9. He stipulates that 'the use of the word *problematics* as a substantive' is 'an indispensable neologism' (Deleuze [1968] 1994: 323).
10. As Coquand says: 'The solution of the problem B must be reduced to the solution of the problem $A \wedge (A \rightarrow B)$. So, suppose a solution of this problem is given. This means that one has both a solution of problem A, and a solution of problem $A \rightarrow B$, i.e. one may reduce the solution of problem B to that of problem A. Hence, as desired, we can solve problem B.

On the other hand, the principle of excluded middle in the form

$$A \vee \neg A$$

can not be justified. Indeed, a solution would be a general method which, given a problem A, would either give a solution or show that a contradiction follows from the assumption that problem A is solvable. As Kolmogorov states, unless one is bold enough to consider oneself omniscient, it must be recognized that there is no solution to this problem' Coquand [2004] 2007: 31–2.
11. Aristotle, *On Interpretation*, ch. 9, 19a[30], trans. G. E. M. Anscombe, in Anscombe 1956.
12. As in *hápax legómenon* (παξ λεγόμενον).
13. With an erroneous pagination. Deleuze writes: '*Science de la logique*, Ed. Aubier, II, p. 277'. But the page is in volume I of this translation by Sandor Jankélévitch.
14. See Hegel [1816] 2010: 213–15.
15. Cf. *The Logic of Sense*, Deleuze [1969] 1990: 339.
16. See Spinoza 1992: § 23.
17. See Deleuze [1968] 1994: 322.
18. See Coquand [2004] 2007: § 1.1.
19. See Deleuze [1968] 1994: 322.
20. See Deleuze [1968] 1994: 322. Albert Lautman (2006) *Les Mathématiques, les idées et le réel physique*, Paris: Vrin. For a general introduction to Lautman, see my review of this re-edition (Dumoncel 2008).
21. 'A problem is determined only by the singular points which express its conditions' (Deleuze [1969] 1990: 54).
22. On the differential equation $w'' + p_1(z)w' + p_2(z)w = 0$.
23. On the differential equation $dy/dx = Q(x, y)/P(x, y)$.
24. See Lautman [2006] 2011: 179–80.
25. More precisely, these two equations are themselves the two *solutions* of an equation.
26. As Deleuze alludes, it is a conception from which Proclus, at least takes his distance.
27. Cf. J. L. Austin (1979) 'The Line and the Cave in Plato's Republic', in *Philosophical Papers*, ed. J. O. Urmson and G. J. Warnock, Oxford: Oxford University Press; J. C. Dumoncel (1992) 'La théorie platonicienne des Idées-Nombres', *Revue de Philosophie Ancienne*, X :1, pp. 1–34, reprinted in J. C. Dumoncel (2002) *La tradition de la* Mathesis Universalis, Paris: Unebévue-éditeur.

References

Anscombe, G. E. M. (1956) 'Aristotle and the Sea Battle', *Mind*, 65:257, pp. 1–15.

Carnot, L. [1881] (1970) *Réflexions sur la métaphysique du calcul infinitésimal*, Paris: Blanchard.

Cavaillès J. [1939] (1946) 'La Pensée mathématique', *Bulletin de la Société Française de Philosophie*, séance du 4 février 1939, tome XL.

Cavaillès, J. (1994) *Œuvres complètes de Philosophie des Sciences*, ed. Bruno Huisman, Paris: Hermann.

Coquand, T. [2004] (2007) 'Kolmogorov's Contribution to Intuitionistic Logic', in E. Charpentier, A. Lesne, and N. K. Nikolski (eds), *Kolmogorov's Heritage in Mathematics*, Berlin and Heidelberg: Springer-Verlag, pp. 19–40.

Deleuze, Gilles [1983] (1986) *Cinema 1: The Movement-Image*, trans. Hugh Tomlinson and Barbara Habberjam, London: Athlone Press.

Deleuze, Gilles [1985] (1989) *Cinema 2: The Time-Image*, trans. Hugh Tomlinson and Robert Galeta, London: Athlone Press.

Deleuze, G. [1969] (1990) *The Logic of Sense*, ed. C. V. Boundas, trans. M. Lester with C. Stivale, London: Athlone Press.

Deleuze, G. [1968] (1994) *Difference and Repetition*, trans. P. Patton, London: Athlone Press.

Deleuze, G. and F. Guattari [1980] (1987) *A Thousand Plateaus*, trans. B. Massumi, Minneapolis: University of Minnesota Press.

Deleuze, G. and F. Guattari [1991] (1994) *What Is Philosophy?*, trans. G. Burchell and H. Tomlinson, New York: Columbia University Press.

Dosse, F. [2007] (2010) *Gilles Deleuze and Félix Guattari: Intersecting Lives*, trans. D. Glassman, New York: Columbia University Press.

Dumoncel, J. C. (2008) 'Review: Lautman, *Les mathématiques, les idées et le réel physique*', in *History and Philosophy of Logic* 29:2, pp. 199–205.

Hegel, G. W. F. [1816] (2010) *The Science of Logic*, trans. G. Di Giovanni, New York: Cambridge University Press.

Hilbert, D. [1923] (1996) 'The Logical Foundations of Mathematics', in W. Ewald (ed.), *From Kant to Hilbert. A Source Book in the Foundations of Mathematics*, vol. 2, Oxford: Oxford University Press, pp. 1134–48.

Lautman, A. [2006] (2011) *Mathematics, Ideas, and the Physical Real*, trans. S. Duffy, London: Continuum.

Leibniz, G. W. [1687] (1978) *Die Philosophischen Schriften von G. W. Leibniz*, vol. 7, ed. C. I. Gerhardt, Hildesheim and New York: Georg Olms Verlag.

Leibniz, G. W. (1981) *New Essays on Human Understanding*, trans. P. Remnant and J. Bennett, Cambridge: Cambridge University Press.

Leibniz, G. W. [1916] (1992) *New Essays Concerning Human Understanding*, vol. IV, trans. A. G. Langley, 2nd edn, La Salle, IL: Open Court Publishing.

Peirce C. S. (1933) 'The Logic of Relatives', in *The Monist (1897), in The Collected Papers, Volume III: Exact Logic and Volume IV: The Simplest Mathematics*, ed. C. Hartshorne and P. Weiss, Cambridge, MA: Harvard University Press.

Peirce, C. S. [1898] (1992) *Reasoning and the Logic of Things*, ed. K. L. Ketner, Cambridge, MA: Harvard University Press.

Peirce, C. S. [1903] (1998) 'Nomenclature and Divisions of Triadic Relations, as Far as They are Determined', in *The Essential Peirce*, vol. 2 (1893–1913), Bloomington: Indiana University Press.

Plato (1921) *Plato: Theaetetus, Sophist. The Loeb Classical Library, L 123*, trans. H. N. Fowle, London: William Heinemann.

Proclus (1970) *A Commentary on the First Book of Euclid's Elements*, Oxford: Princeton University Press.

Spinoza, B. (1992) *The Ethics, Treatise on the Emendation of the Intellect, and Selected Letters*, ed. S. Feldman, trans. S. Shirley, Indiana: Hackett Publishing.

Deleuze's Third Synthesis of Time[1]

Daniela Voss   Free University of Berlin

Abstract

Deleuze's theory of time set out in *Difference and Repetition* is a complex structure of three different syntheses of time – the passive synthesis of the living present, the passive synthesis of the pure past and the static synthesis of the future. This article focuses on Deleuze's third synthesis of time, which seems to be the most obscure part of his tripartite theory, as Deleuze mixes different theoretical concepts drawn from philosophy, Greek drama theory and mathematics. Of central importance is the notion of the cut, which is constitutive of the third synthesis of time defined as an a priori ordered temporal series separated unequally into a before and an after. This article argues that Deleuze develops his *ordinal* definition of time with recourse to Kant's definition of time as pure and empty form, Hölderlin's notion of 'caesura' drawn from his 'Remarks on *Oedipus*' (1803) and Dedekind's method of cuts as developed in his pioneering essay 'Continuity and Irrational Numbers' (1872). Deleuze then ties together the conceptions of the Kantian empty form of time and the Nietzschean eternal return, both of which are essentially related to a fractured I or dissolved self. This article aims to assemble the different heterogeneous elements that Deleuze picks up on and to show how the third synthesis of time emerges from this differential multiplicity.

Keywords: synthesis of time, Kant, Hölderlin, Dedekind, eternal return

I. Kant's Definition of Time

In his 1978 lecture series on Kantian philosophy, Deleuze states what seemed to be most essential to him: 'all of the creations and novelties

Deleuze Studies 7.2 (2013): 194–216
DOI: 10.3366/dls.2013.0102
© Edinburgh University Press
www.euppublishing.com/dls

that Kantianism will bring to philosophy turn on a certain problem of time and an entirely new conception of time' (Deleuze 1978a: 1). According to Deleuze, Kant's greatest achievement is the radical reversal of previous cosmological and psychological conceptions of time. With Kant, time is no longer subordinated to the measure of movements in nature (such as the movement of celestial bodies in their orbits), nor can it be defined by the simple succession of psychological states. Instead, Kant defines time as a 'form of interiority', a pure and empty form, in which all change of appearances is to be thought, but which does not change itself. In Deleuze's words, time loses its modal character and ceases to be cyclical. It becomes a pure straight line that cleaves the subject into two unequal halves: the empirico-transcendental doublet. Referring to these novelties that Kantianism brings to the philosophy of time, Deleuze chooses two poetic formulas: (1) 'The time is out of joint', uttered by Hamlet in Shakespeare's tragedy *Hamlet, Prince of Denmark*, and (2) 'I is an Other' from the French poet Rimbaud.[2] In what way do these poetic formulas apply to Kant's theory of time?

(1) Hamlet's utterance 'The time is out of joint' refers to a particular time, that is, the time through which he is living. However, in the way that Deleuze uses the formula it has a much wider, metaphysical import: 'Time out of joint' now means that time has become 'demented time' (*temps affolé*), it has lost its balance, its groundedness, its stability, which it still possessed in ancient Greek cosmology. According to Plato, time presented a 'moving image of eternity' (Plato 1997: 37d), which moved according to number. For both Plato and Aristotle, time was defined as a 'number of movement', counted by the celestial revolution of planets passing through certain 'cardinal points'. The uniform and circular motion of planets provided a means to mark off regular periods of time. Consequently, time was thought of as cyclical and inseparable from the movement of physical bodies. As Aristotle put it: 'time is a number of movement – but there is no movement without physical body' (Aristotle 1995: 279a15). This is why Deleuze attributes to the ancient Greeks a concept of time which 'is a mode and not a being. No more than number is a being, it's a mode in relation to what it quantifies, in the same way time is a mode in relation to what it measures' (Deleuze 1978b: 2). According to Deleuze, time loses its modal character and ceases to be circular only subsequent to the establishment of modern science in the sixteenth and seventeenth centuries (in particular, in the scientific cosmology of Newton). With Kant finally, time becomes purely formal, it has unrolled itself into a pure 'straight line'. As we will see, the consequences of this new Kantian definition of time are tremendous: the

ancient cosmological harmony between the world and the heavens, man and the heavenly gods has broken down. Time has ceased to be an image of the eternal order. It has shaken off its subordination to the periodical movements of planets. It is as though Timaeus's prediction has become true: 'Be that as it may, Time came into being together with the Heaven, in order that, as they were brought into being together, so they may be dissolved together, if ever their dissolution should come to pass' (Plato 1997: 38b). The time of antiquity has perished together with the gods and the heavens, and a new time is born. Pure and empty time is now the true subjectivity. It has become an infinite, straight line, which cuts right through the consciousness of the modern subject.

(2) Deleuze expresses this fracture of the modern subject with Rimbaud's formula 'I is an Other'. This is then the second novelty that Kant brings to philosophy by uncovering 'that schizophrenia in principle' (Deleuze 1994: 58). By defining time as a form of interiority, Kant introduces a fundamental split in the subject. The Kantian subject is torn between the form of spontaneity, that is, the 'I think' which accompanies all concept production and guarantees the unity of synthesis, and the empirical self which experiences the effects of thought rather than initiating the act of thought itself. According to Deleuze, Rimbaud's formula 'I is an Other' is apt to express the alienation to which the Kantian subject succumbs. It should be noted, however, that Rimbaud's phrase occurs in a rather different context. Rimbaud understands the formula 'I is an Other' in the light of Aristotle's distinction between determining form and indeterminate matter. This becomes evident, when Rimbaud says: 'Too bad for the wood which finds itself a violin! If the copper wakes up a bugle, that is not its fault' (Deleuze 1984: ix).[3] By means of the formula 'I is an Other', Rimbaud expresses the experience of being formed by thought rather than being the originator. Thought forms me – I am not the master of thought at all.

With Kant, however, the concern is no longer of a form that informs matter but – in Deleuze's words – of 'an infinite modulation, no longer a mould' (Deleuze 1984: ix). *Thought works within me*. I am affected by thought that is both mine and the thought of an Other. The fracture or crack in the 'I' is produced by the pure and empty form of time. This means that I experience myself, that is, my feelings, thoughts, actions and bodily sensations, always under the condition of time, which is the interior form of receptivity. But the synthesis of all these different representations within the unity of consciousness is performed by the transcendental I, or the 'I think' as the transcendental form of apperception. Phrased more precisely, the I affects itself under the form of time. The remarkable outcome of this kind of auto-affection is that the difference between being and thought, or matter and form, is *interiorised*. Deleuze refers to this establishment of internal difference as the moment of 'discovery of the transcendental, the element of the Copernican Revolution' (Deleuze 1994: 86). Thus, for Deleuze, the transcendental difference that Kant discovers is necessarily linked to his definition of time as form of interiority or form of auto-affection which splits the subject into two unequal halves: the empirico-transcendental doublet.

II. Hölderlin's Caesura

Certainly, Deleuze does not simply adopt the Kantian empirico-transcendental doublet with its distinctive distribution of active synthesis and passive receptivity without synthesis. What he takes up instead is the idea of an internal difference or fracture in the subject, which occurs through the disruptive introduction of a caesura or cut. Deleuze's account of the third synthesis of time deviates from the Kantian definition of time as an a priori given, infertile subjective form. Instead, Deleuze conceives of time as a productive power of synthesis – in his words, a 'static synthesis' which is constituted by a 'caesura' or cut. He finds the notion of the 'caesura' in Greek drama theory, more concretely, in Hölderlin's 'Remarks on *Oedipus*'.

Hölderlin interprets Sophocles's *Oedipus Rex* as the undoing of the coupling between man and god: man and god have become 'an unlimited One', which, however, can be 'purified' only through an 'unlimited separation' (Hölderlin 1969: 736). Deleuze describes this unlimited separation as a double deviation: 'God turns away from man who turns away from God' (Deleuze 1978b: 4). While in the tragedies of Aeschylus or Euripides the gods still ensured justice, they punished and pardoned according to their judgement, Sophocles's tragedy marks a significant change. The bond between man and the gods has broken. The gods abandon Oedipus in the critical moment of his suffering, and Oedipus rages against the divine betrayal, searching desperately for who he is and trying to recover his identity. Hölderlin describes the moment as follows:

> In the utmost form of suffering... there exists nothing but the conditions of time and space. Inside it, man forgets himself because he exists entirely for the moment, the god [forgets himself] because he is nothing but time; and either one is unfaithful, time, because it is reversed categorically at such a moment, and beginning and end no longer rhyme; man because at this moment of

categorical reversal he has to follow and thus can no longer resemble the beginning in what follows. (Hölderlin 1969: 736)

Oedipus is left with the pure form of time, which is emptied of all meaningful content and announces neither punishment nor relief from the interminable, incessant suffering. As Hölderlin says, time is reversed categorically: it no longer forms a cycle in which beginning and end rhyme – as it was still the case in the tragedies of Aeschylus and Euripides, when the unity of the cosmos was intact, and when the divine law revealed itself in the order of the universe, the course of nature and human fate. Now, the cycle of time has unrolled itself and become a straight line, the tortuous, indivisible and incessant labyrinth that Deleuze finds in Borges (Deleuze 1984: vii, 1978b: 2).[4] It is the straight line that Oedipus wanders in his long and lonesome wandering through the desert with no aim and no end in sight. As Hölderlin says in very Kantian terms, 'there exists nothing but the conditions of time and space' (Hölderlin 1969: 736).[5]

Moreover, when Oedipus's crime is finally discovered, that is, when the blind seer Tiresias reveals to Oedipus that he had killed his own father Laius and married his own mother Jocasta of Thebes, Oedipus can no longer resemble what he has been before. Tiresias's intervention has put before Oedipus the thought that he may not be the son of King Polybus of Corinth and his wife Merope who raised him. This is a thought which is almost impossible to think. All of the personal memories in which Oedipus has believed so far, together with his future expectations are eliminated, destroyed at a single blow. In fact, the caesura is not only a break in time, but also a split of Oedipus's self. Oedipus is other to himself. He experiences this internal difference in the pure present, the 'pureness' of which signifies that it occurs like a cut. The series of former presents do not converge with this present moment.

We thus have an order of time, determined by the caesura which draws together a before and an after and thereby the totality of time. It is of little importance when the caesura, that is, the exact moment of the fracture of the self, happens in empirical time. It can be at the moment of Tiresias's revelation or a little later after Oedipus's further inquiries. Or a crack might have appeared when Oedipus committed the crime of killing his father and then marrying his mother. To complicate things further, maybe an invisible crack already became manifest when the infant Oedipus was saved from death against the will of his father and in defiance of the gods' oracle. The empirical incarnation does not count: the caesura or cut refers to a symbolic event, which determines the order of time a priori. Thus, the past is the time before the caesura; the pure present is the becoming equal to the event and the experience of internal difference; the future finally is the time after the caesura.

III. Dedekind's Method of Cuts

As we have seen, Deleuze's third synthesis of time has to be understood as an *a priori ordered series* that is produced by a caesura. The caesura is the formal element which distributes on both sides the before and the after which no longer rhyme together. Deleuze insists that

> the future and the past here are not empirical and dynamic determinations of time: they are formal and fixed characteristics which follow *a priori* from the order of time, as though they comprised a static synthesis of time. The synthesis is necessarily static, since time is no longer subordinated to movement; time is the most radical form of change, but the form of change does not change. (Deleuze 1994: 89)

The idea of the form of time, which does not change itself, is clearly a Kantian thought. Repeatedly, Kant says in the *Critique of Pure Reason* that 'time itself does not alter, but only something that is within time' (Kant 1998: A41/B58).[6] But is it true that Deleuze still adheres to the traditional philosophical conception of form? Deleuze's remarks on a 'static synthesis' should make us suspect that Deleuze is not simply repeating Kant's theory here. Equally, the idea of a 'caesura', which constitutes a serial and linear time by distributing a before and an after, indicates a source other than Kant. For sure, Deleuze deduces the term 'caesura' first and foremost from Greek drama theory, but in his lecture course on Kant of 21 March 1978, he does not hesitate to compare it to the mathematical terms 'limit' and 'cut' (*coupure*).[7] Moreover, the word 'caesura' derives from the Latin root '*caes*' and can thus be rendered as 'cut'.[8] For these reasons, we suggest that the 'caesura' can be understood by means of the concept of 'cut' in Dedekind's theory of real numbers, which Deleuze discusses in Chapter 4 of *Difference and Repetition* in the context of the continuousness of Ideas (Deleuze 1994: 172).

The mathematician Richard Dedekind (1831–1916) is famous for giving a rigorous arithmetical foundation to differential calculus, and thereby expunging from calculus geometric undefined concepts such as 'infinitesimal' quantities and the limit concept involving the idea of *approaching*. Deleuze acknowledges his achievements, in particular the renewed conception of limit: 'the limit no longer presupposes the ideas of a continuous variable and infinite approximation. On the contrary, the notion of limit grounds a new, static and purely ideal definition of continuity' (Deleuze 1994: 172). Indeed, it can be argued that Dedekind invents this new 'static and purely ideal' conception of continuity. His thoughts on continuity were first published in the groundbreaking essay 'Continuity and Irrational Numbers' in 1872, fourteen years after he developed the basic ideas on which it relies. The main question the essay deals with is: what is the nature of continuity? As Dedekind states:

> an explanation of this continuity is nowhere given; even the most rigorous expositions of the differential calculus do not base their proofs upon continuity but... they either appeal to geometric notions or those suggested by geometry, or depend upon theorems which are never established in a purely arithmetic manner. (Dedekind 1901a: 2)

That is, the notion of continuity was either geometrically explained as a vague hang-togetherness, an 'unbroken connection in the smallest parts' (Dedekind 1901a: 10–11) or was based on insufficiently founded theorems, such as that every magnitude which grows continually, but not beyond all limits, must certainly approach a limiting value. Dedekind set himself the task of securing a real definition of the essence of continuity. He first approached the problem by trying to 'map' the geometrical continuum (the straight line) onto ordered systems of discrete quantities (numbers). Comparing the system of rational numbers with the points of the straight line, he saw that they cannot be put into a one-to-one-correspondence with each other: although each rational number can be correlated with a point on the line, not every point of the line can be expressed as a rational number. In fact, in the straight line there are infinitely many points which correspond to no rational number. To identify these points, which are inexpressible as rational numbers, Dedekind used a method of division: the Dedekind 'cuts' (*Schnitte*). Any cut divides the points of the line into two classes, such that all the points of one class are always to the left of all the points of the other. Furthermore, there is precisely one and only one point determined by this cut. The cut can correspond to a rational number, or else designate a 'gap' between the rational numbers, that is, an irrational quantity (such as $\sqrt{2}$). In the latter case, cuts define a new type of number, that is, the irrational numbers.

Dedekind first made use of geometrical considerations in order to introduce the notion of the cut. However, he sought to define cuts directly in terms of the number system, so that any reflections on geometric lines can be put aside. As Robert Bunn says:

Geometry was to serve only as the source of the idea for constructing an arithmetical foundation. The continuous system which was to be Dedekind's foundation would be arithmetical in the sense that its operations would ultimately be defined in terms of operations on natural numbers, and no mention would be made of any geometrical objects. (Bunn 1980: 223)

Dedekind demanded that the system of rational numbers be improved by 'the creation of new numbers such that the domain of numbers shall gain the same completeness, or as we may say at once, the same *continuity*, as the straight line' (Dedekind 1901a: 9). As it is, the system of rational numbers is marked by a certain incompleteness or discontinuity, due to the existence of gaps. Thus, in order to render the domain of rational numbers into a continuous system, Dedekind defined for each cut that is not produced by a rational number a 'new object', which he called an irrational number. For example, $\sqrt{2}$ can be defined as the cut between two classes, A and B, where A contains all those numbers whose squares are less than two and B those whose squares are greater than two.

It should be noted that Dedekind did not identify irrational numbers with cuts, since every definite cut produces either a definite rational or irrational number. Rather, Dedekind cuts constitute 'the next genus of numbers' (Deleuze 1994: 172), namely 'real numbers'. The order of real numbers allows the treatment of both rational and irrational numbers as elements in an encompassing number system, which forms a continuous and ordered system. It has to be emphasised that this continuity of the number system is something quite different from the traditional conception of continuity founded on the intuition of the way in which geometric quantities arise: according to an intuitive conception of continuity, a line is considered continuous insofar as it arises from the continuous movement of a point, and a plane from the movement of a line. By contrast, Dedekind's new conception of continuity claims not to rely on intuition, or any considerations of smooth movement. It claims to contain nothing empirical, since it can be deduced from number systems alone. For Dedekind, 'numbers are free creations of the human mind' (Dedekind 1901b: 31). As he explained in his 1888 essay 'The Nature and Meaning of Numbers' (*Was sind und was sollen die Zahlen?*):

> In speaking of arithmetic (algebra, analysis) as a part of logic I mean to imply that I consider the number-concept entirely independent of the notions or intuitions of space and time, that I consider it an immediate result from the laws of thought. (Dedekind 1901b: 31)

Accordingly, Dedekind's project of arithmetising the conception of continuity was not to be grounded on vague, geometrical intuitions of space and time but rather on an Idea of reason: the Idea of an infinite, ordered and dense set of numbers each of which can in principle be identified by a Dedekind cut.[9] In fact, Dedekind's 'continuity' can better be described as the property of the 'completeness' that characterises certain densely ordered number systems. As Robert Bunn puts it:

a densely ordered system is *complete* (*continuous*) in Dedekind's sense if every cut in the system is produced by exactly one element of the system, that is, if there is an element of the system which is either the maximum of the lower section or the minimum of the upper section. (Bunn 1980: 222)

Bunn concludes that 'the term "continuous" is not an especially apt one for the characteristic involved, but it indicated the correlate in the old system – continuous magnitude' (Bunn 1980: 222). Carl Boyer, a historian of mathematics, explains that the notion of continuity 'specifies only *an infinite, discrete multiplicity of elements*, satisfying certain conditions – that the set be ordered, dense, and perfect' (Boyer 1949: 294; emphasis added), whereby the mathematical term 'perfect' is synonymous with the term 'complete', which are both translations of the German term '*vollkommen*'. Boyer further argues that there is 'nothing dynamic in the idea of continuity' (Boyer 1949: 294).

However, it is not altogether clear whether Dedekind really succeeded in giving a purely ideal, arithmetic definition of continuity. In fact, he is criticised by Russell and Wittgenstein for failing to get away from the geometrical image of the number line.[10] Russell argues that Dedekind's method of dividing all the terms of a series into two classes, one greater than the cut and one less than the cut, proves problematic in the case where the point of section is supposed to represent an irrational. In this case, the two classes of either side of the cut have no limit or last term. For instance, in the case of the irrational section at $\sqrt{2}$, 'there is no maximum to the ratios whose square is less than 2, and no minimum to those whose square is greater than 2.... Between these two classes, where $\sqrt{2}$ ought to be, there is nothing' (Russell 1919: 68). Thus, a 'gap' appears at the point of section where the irrational is supposed to be. According to Russell, the spatial image of a line and the unsettling idea of a gap led people to postulate that there must be some limit:

From the habit of being influenced by spatial imagination, people have supposed that series *must* have limits in cases where it seems odd if they do not. Thus, perceiving that there was no rational limit to the ratios whose square is less than 2, they allowed themselves to 'postulate' an *irrational* limit, which was to fill the Dedekind gap. Dedekind, in the above-mentioned work ['Continuity and Irrational Numbers'], set up the axiom that the gap must always be filled, *i.e.* that every section must have a boundary. (Russell 1919: 71)

Russell condemns this method of 'postulating' and aims to give a precise definition of real numbers by a method of 'construction' (Russell 1919: 73). That is, he abandons the idea of points of space or extension and substitutes for them the logical construction of 'segments'. He finds that 'segments of rational numbers... fulfil all the requirements laid down in Cantor's definition, and also those derived from the principle of abstraction. Hence there is no logical ground for distinguishing segments of rationals from real numbers' (Russell 1937: § 270).[11]

Wittgenstein joins Russell in his criticism of Dedekind's method of cuts, although he does not follow Russell's set-theoretical solution. According to Wittgenstein, the major error that Dedekind committed was using the concept of cut – a concept which is *taken over from the everyday use of language* and that is why it immediately looks as it if had to have a meaning for numbers too' (Wittgenstein 1956: 150; original emphasis). The verb 'cutting' is commonly used to refer to an activity that divides a spatially extended object into parts. The cutting of a number line is supposed to work analogously: the division produced is seen 'under the aspect of a cut made somewhere along the straight line, *hence extensionally*' (149; original emphasis). 'The cut is an extensional *image*' (150; original emphasis). For Wittgenstein, the idea of a cut is 'a dangerous illustration' and yields only an 'imaginary', a 'fanciful application' (148). However, Wittgenstein admits that in a way we can attach a meaning to the expression that every rational number is a principle of division of the rational numbers (149), but this is not so in the case of irrationals, which are not even defined as numbers yet. From the erroneous image of a number line the idea ensues that irrationals can be represented as points on the line just like the rationals, and that both are elements of an encompassing number system, the real numbers. 'The misleading thing about Dedekind's conception', Wittgenstein says, 'is the idea that the real numbers are there spread out in the number line' (151). 'The picture of the number line is an absolutely natural one up to a certain point; that is to say so long as it is not used for a general theory of real numbers' (148). Wittgenstein faults Dedekind for his general way of talking, which, although it might prove useful, implies 'the danger... that one will think one is in possession of the complete explanation of the individual cases' (153). Thus, we are led to believe that 'the *general* account could be quite understood even without examples, without a thought of intension*s* (in the plural), since really everything could be managed extensionally' (153; original emphasis). The problem with irrationals surely is that no example of an irrational number could really be given. The ancient Pythagorean example of the square root of two again relies on a geometrical illustration, namely the square's diagonal, which proves incommensurable with the square's sides whose lengths measure one unit. Within this geometrical image, the square root of two can be represented by the intersection of a circular arc (generated by taking the diagonal as the radius of a circle) and the straight line extending from the square's base. However, by what right can we say that this intersection identifies a point and defines a number? As Wittgenstein hypothetically suggests: 'For, if I were to construct really accurately, then the circle would have to cut the straight line *between* its points', and he continues: 'This is a frightfully confusing picture' (151; original emphasis). We almost feel forced to assign to the irrational a point on the line, because we are in the grip of a picture (the picture of a continuous straight line consisting of points). However, why can we not define the irrational as a number? The expression $\sqrt{2}$ certainly seems to indicate a number, yet what it does is simply to provide a rule for generating an indefinitely expanding decimal fraction. For Wittgenstein, irrationals are rules or laws; they do not indicate some Platonic arithmetical entity, a perfectly definite number, but rather 'the unlimited technique of expansion of series' (144).

As we have seen, both Russell and Wittgenstein doubt that Dedekind managed to escape the geometric image of the number line in his attempt to provide a purely arithmetic definition of irrationals. Let us now bring Deleuze into the discussion. It seems that Deleuze does not have qualms about Dedekind's method of cuts and definition of continuity. Indeed, he says that we gain 'a new, static and purely ideal definition of continuity' (Deleuze 1994: 172), which is grounded on the Dedekind cut, inasmuch as it constitutes this new continuous and ordered system of real numbers. Deleuze also calls the Dedekind cut the 'ideal cause of continuity' (Deleuze 1994: 172). Now the question to ask is: in what way can Deleuze benefit from Dedekind's theory of cuts and the notion of continuity that designates not a 'vague hang-togetherness' but rather an infinite, discrete multiplicity of elements whose order is a priori determined? Deleuze uses Dedekind's ideas in order to construct a time that is not empirically defined through our intuition of a dynamic flux of events, but one that is determined a priori and designates a *static state of affairs*. This latter time is a 'static synthesis' of discrete elements (past and future moments), which are distributed by the caesura, that is, 'a genuine cut (*coupure*)' (Deleuze 1994: 172), into a before and an after.

The caesura or cut is constitutive of this continuous ordered system of time, which maps onto the straight line. Thus, Deleuze transforms the Kantian definition of a purely formal time by means of mathematical considerations on the notion of 'cut' and 'static synthesis'. For Deleuze, the third synthesis of time is not simply an a priori subjective form, but an a priori and a-subjective static synthesis of a multiplicity of temporal series.

However, Deleuze's account of a serial and linear time is not as straightforward as we have presented it above. Deleuze does indeed make use of the Dedekind cut and the idea that it constitutes a static continuum, yet he takes licence in modifying Dedekind in a way that is not Dedekindian at all. The way that Deleuze conceives the series of time rather incorporates the idea of the irrational cut designating a 'gap'.[12] In *Difference and Repetition*, Deleuze says that 'the irrational numbers... differ in kind from the terms of the series of rational numbers' (Deleuze 1994: 172). They are 'constructed on the basis of an essential inequality' in relation to the next-lowest type of numbers, that is, the rational numbers. That is to say, they express the 'impossibility of determining a common aliquot part for two quantities, and thus the impossibility of reducing their relation to even a fractional number' (232). However, they compensate for their characteristic inequality by their 'limit-equality indicated by a convergent series of rational numbers' (232).[13] Now the interesting move by Deleuze is to ascribe an original intensive nature to irrationals, an implication of difference or inequality, which is cancelled or covered over as soon as they are constructed as elements of an extensive plane of rational numbers. In fact, Deleuze holds that an intensive nature belongs to every type of number, insofar as they are not explicated, developed and equalised in an extensity:

> Every number is originally intensive and vectorial in so far as it implies a difference of quantity which cannot properly be cancelled, but extensive and scalar in so far as it cancels this difference on another plane that it creates and on which it is explicated. (Deleuze 1994: 232)

Deleuze's claim that irrationals have a certain intensive depth, an inequality or implicated difference, which is cancelled in the general definition of a continuum of real numbers, seems to resonate with Wittgenstein's remark: 'The extensional definitions of functions, real numbers etc. pass over – although they presuppose – everything intensional, and refer to the ever-recurring outward form' (Wittgenstein 1956: 150). However, while Wittgenstein seems to understand the 'intensional' nature rather in terms of a rule or law, Deleuze speaks of 'intensity' and its differential nature.[14]

Deleuze's reflections on the nature of irrationals show that he also regards the number line as a fiction, a spatial image, which covers over an intensive depth. The straight line of rational points is but 'a false infinity, a simple undefinite that includes an infinity of lacunae; that is why the continuous is a labyrinth that cannot be represented by a straight line' (Deleuze 1993: 17). We have already come across Borges's labyrinth of the straight line. Thus, it seems that Deleuze, when he speaks of a line of time, does not mean a simple straight line, but one that is perforated by lacunae.[15] These lacunae or gaps are precisely designated by the irrational cut, that is, the interstice between series of rational numbers. They symbolise the irruption of the virtual event within the empirical continuum of space and the chronological succession of instants.

In order to better understand the impact of the cut, that is, the irruption of the virtual event on the subject, we have to turn to Nietzsche. As will become clear, all threads come together with Nietzsche's eternal return.[16] In Deleuze's reading, the eternal return is a *series of time*, constituted by an irrational cut, 'which brings together the before and the after in a becoming' (Deleuze 1989: 155). This irrational cut or caesura produces a split subject and brings it into contact with an outside, the realm of virtual events. In fact, in *Cinema 2*, Deleuze explicitly connects the concept of the irrational cut with Nietzsche's conception of time in his definition of the third time-image:

> This time-image puts thought into contact with an unthought, the unsummonable, the inexplicable, the undecidable, the incommensurable. The outside or the obverse of the images has replaced the whole, at the same time as the interstice or the cut has replaced association. (Deleuze 1989: 214)[17]

IV. Nietzsche's Eternal Return

The cut or caesura of serial time has a detrimental impact on the subject. We have already seen that Deleuze's third synthesis of time is profoundly linked to the notion of a fractured I, be it Kant's empirico-transcendental doublet or Oedipus's dissolved self, as developed in Hölderlin. Now Deleuze turns to Nietzsche, who will be the last and most important philosopher in this Deleuzian line-up of great thinkers. Nietzsche's eternal return will be defined as a series of time, which is cut by a unique and tremendous event, namely 'the death of God [that] becomes effective only with the dissolution of the Self' (Deleuze

1994: 58). However, as will become clear, the eternal return does not only have a destructive and lethal impact, rather it manifests a positive and productive power. It carries the ungrounded and abandoned subject to a point of metamorphosis, when all its possibilities of becoming are set free. It liberates the subject not only from the rule of identity and law, but also from the form of the true and thus bestows it with the power of the false and its artistic, creative potential. As we will see in this section, the dissolved self becomes Nietzsche's aesthetic concept of the overman, who is capable of affirming difference and becoming.

It should be noted that Nietzsche never fully laid out his thought of the eternal return in his writings and that the existing interpretations in secondary literature vary to a great extent. What interests us here is solely Deleuze's reconstruction of the eternal return, which is considerably influenced, as we will see, by Pierre Klossowski's reading of Nietzsche.[18]

According to Deleuze, the thought of the eternal return is not to be understood as a return of the Same or the Similar. Rather, what passes the test of the eternal return is that which differs internally, simulacra or the dissolved self. The eternal return has to be seen as a test of selection, which banishes identity, that is, the identity of God, the identity of the world or the represented object, and the coherence of the self. Thus, the landscape of the eternal return is that of difference-in-itself, the irreducibly unequal, of metamorphosis or becoming. In Deleuze's words:

> Essentially, the unequal, the different is the true rationale for the eternal return. It is because nothing is equal, or the same, that 'it' comes back. In other words, the eternal return is predicated only of becoming and the multiple. It is the law of a world without being, without unity, without identity. (Deleuze 2004: 124)

Therefore, in a first move, it is important to distinguish Nietzsche's eternal return from the conception of a 'return of the Same and the Similar' which is the essence of a cyclical conception of time. Thus, the ancient Greeks presupposed an identity or resemblance in general of all the instances that are supposed to recur. They regarded the recurrence of planetary motion, the uniform change of seasons and qualitative changes in things as laws of nature. According to Deleuze, Nietzsche's thought of the eternal return cannot be presented as a natural law and identified with the ancient Greek hypothesis of cyclical time.[19] First, he argues that as a connoisseur of the Greeks, Nietzsche could not have been ignorant of the Greek hypothesis of time as a cycle. Thus, when Nietzsche insists that his thought of the eternal return is something effectively *new*, we have to take him seriously. Furthermore, Nietzsche is a thinker who is very much opposed to the notion of law. He would not have submitted to the simple notion of a law of nature. As textual evidence, one can adduce two passages in *Zarathustra*, where Nietzsche explicitly rejects the interpretation of the eternal return as cyclical time: (1) during the encounter between Zarathustra and the dwarf, the dwarf says, 'All truth is crooked; time itself is a circle', whereupon Zarathustra replies, 'Thou spirit of gravity!... do not take it too lightly' (Nietzsche 1936: 167); (2) on another occasion, Zarathustra rebukes his animals that they have already made a 'refrain' out of his doctrine of the eternal return. In a refrain, the same always returns, but apparently Zarathustra does not want the eternal return be understood as a refrain (see Nietzsche 1936: 234).

In what way, then, is the eternal return different from a natural cycle, a cycle of time? The crucial issue is that the eternal return is *selective* and *creative*. It is selective with regard to desires or thought and with regard to being. Let us first consider its mechanism of selection with regard to desires. If the doctrine of the eternal return is stated in terms of an ethical rule, it becomes a sort of Kantian imperative: 'Whatever you will, you have to will it in such a way that you will its eternal return.' That which is expelled by the selection test of the eternal return is all instances of willing that want a thing only for once: 'only this one time'. In an unpublished note contemporaneous with *The Gay Science*, Nietzsche says that it does not matter whether the act I am about to perform is informed by ambition, or laziness, or obedience, if only I re-will my present action again, for innumerable times.[20] The eternal return excludes any half-hearted willing and affirms the extreme forms: it separates an active, superior will, which wants to enact its force to its highest power, from a reactive, gregarious will. Moreover, the eternal return not only excludes any 'half-desires' but also any reactive mode of being (such as the passive small man or last man possessed by a will to revenge). Furthermore, it is necessary to note that the superior forms of willing and being do not simply pre-exist the eternal return, but are *created* by the eternal return. In other words, the eternal return is more than a 'theoretical representation' (Deleuze 1994: 41) or ethical rule to be made a self-chosen principle of life. Rather, it is a positive principle that actively creates the superior forms that pass the test of eternal return.

In his book *Nietzsche and the Vicious Circle* (1997), Pierre Klossowski offers an interpretation of the selective and creative power of eternal return. According to Klossowski's analysis, the thought of the eternal return jeopardises the subject's identity; it is an aggression against the apparently limited and closed whole of the subject. The reason for this is that the thought of the eternal return demands that I re-will myself again for innumerable times, but this demand makes me at the same time fall into incoherence. In relation to the codes of everyday society, I am a particular identifiable individual, *once and for all* determined by laws, contractual relations and institutions. The thought of the eternal return addresses me but at the same time demands my destruction as this particular identifiable individual. This is so because I have to re-will *all* my prior possibilities of being:

> All that remains, then, is for me to re-will myself, no longer as the outcome of these prior possibilities, no longer as one realization among thousands, but as a fortuitous moment whose very fortuity implies the necessity of the integral return of the whole series. (Klossowski 1997: 58)
> I deactualize my present self in order to will myself in *all the other selves whose entire series must be passed through*. (Klossowski 1997: 57; original emphasis)

Thus, the eternal return does not demand that I return the same as I am, 'once and for all' (this would amount to a 'bare repetition' in Deleuzian terms), but as a variation, a simulacrum, for an infinite number of times (this would be a repetition 'by excess, the repetition of the future as eternal return' (Deleuze 1994: 90)). The coherence of the subject is thus jeopardised. Nietzsche himself suffered the consequences of the thought of the eternal return: 'I am every name in history,'[21] 'Dionysus and the Crucified.'[22] In Deleuze's reading, which coincides with Klossowski's interpretation in this regard, 'the thinker, undoubtedly the thinker of the eternal return, is . . . the universal individual' (254). For Deleuze, the universal individual or the 'man without a name' (91) designates someone who has relinquished the well-defined identity of the subject with fixed boundaries, and affirmed the system of a dissolved self with all its processes of becoming.

The dissolution of the identity of the subject and the advent of a non-identical, dissolved self has become possible with the death of God. The cut or caesura in Nietzsche's eternal return coincides therefore with the symbolic event of the killing of God. In *The Gay Science*, Nietzsche describes the act of killing God as a deed that is almost 'too great for us', and yet we have done it ourselves. However, according to Nietzsche, the tremendous event has not yet reached the eyes and ears of men. That is, the absence of God, who hitherto guaranteed the identity of the subject by creating man in his own image, ruling him according to divine laws, and securing the immortality of the soul, has not yet become effective. The moment this happens, the identity of the subject will be destroyed. The future marks the time when the excessive event turns back against the subject, dispersing it in a discrete multiplicity of little selves, of egos with many names or, what amounts to the same thing, a universal ego with no name at all:

> What the self has become equal to is the unequal in itself. In this manner, the I which is fractured according to the order of time and the Self which is divided according to the temporal series correspond and find a common descendant in the man without name, without family, without qualities, without self or I, the 'plebeian' guardian of a secret, the already-Overman whose scattered members gravitate around the sublime image. (Deleuze 1994: 90)

The universal individual or man without name is thus to be understood as Nietzsche's overman. The overman is not another higher species of man, but a non-identical, a dissolved self, which is liberated from the judgement of God and open to intensive processes of becoming. Interpretations that regard the overman as 'an evolutionary product, rising higher – as man does relative to the worm – to some indeterminate evolutionary height from which he can look back, amused, at that from which he came' (Grosz 2004: 148), treat the overman as someone beyond man, a higher species that is not yet present. In our view, Deleuze's reading rather suggests that the overman is someone who is always beyond himself, that is, never identical with himself, and who allows for all possibilities of becoming, as Klossowski says, becoming stone, becoming plant, becoming animal, becoming star (Klossowski 1963: 223). Deleuze takes up this thought and states that the thinker of the eternal return 'is laden with stones and diamonds, plants "and even animals"' (Deleuze 1994: 254). Features of the overman can in fact be found in the artist or poet – in short, someone who is willing to undergo metamorphoses and to become-other in favour of an act or a work yet to come. As Deleuze explains in his concluding paper given at the Nietzsche conference in the Royaumont Abbey in July 1964:

> The overman very much resembles the poet as Rimbaud defines it: one who is 'loaded with humanity, even with animals,' and who in every case has retained only the superior form, and the extreme power. (Deleuze 2004: 125; translation modified)

Another suitable example besides the poet or artist might be the political subject, someone who engages in processes that not only demand a becoming-other, that is, an annihilation of the past self that he or she was, but that also put the existence of a future self at risk and thus leave the process of becoming open to success or failure. The ancient rhetorical practice of *parrhesia* can serve as an example here: *parrhesia* can be translated as 'the telling of the unvarnished truth' and specifies a type of discourse in which the speaker commits himself to a free and unbound speech and in doing this puts himself at considerable risk, including the risk of death.[23] The *parrhesiast* or 'truth-teller' cannot be defined in terms of a self-authoring subject, but must be understood as a split subject: through his words he constitutes himself as the one who speaks freely and who is willing to pay for it with his life. He forsakes the identity and securities of his past self, and projects an ideal future self that would find the approval of his listeners, but his project might just as well end in failure.

All these examples, the poet or artist and the political subject (for example, the *parrhesiast*) can be seen as instantiations of a dissolved self, or the overman in Nietzschean terms. Thus, the overman is a real possibility or even a present reality, if one thinks the thought of the eternal return and wills oneself through the *entire series of all the other selves*, that is, affirms all possibilities of becoming. What is expelled by the wheel of eternal return and its centrifugal force is only that which desperately clings to its identity.

V. Conclusion

Deleuze's account of the third synthesis of time involves different theories from philosophy, Greek drama theory and mathematics. It is important to note that Deleuze's method of mixing theoretical concepts is not to be conceived in terms of assimilating differences and blending one concept into the other. Rather, Deleuze maintains their heterogeneity and relates them to one another as differences. It can be regarded as a technique of montage operating by cuts commonly used in cinema. In his second cinema book, Deleuze analyses the time-image of modern cinema with the mathematical terms of incommensurables and irrational cuts (adding, however, the particular meaning of an irrational cut as an irreducible 'gap' and independent 'intensity'):

> The modern image initiates the reign of 'incommensurables' or irrational cuts: this is to say that the cut no longer forms part of one or the other image, of one or the other sequence that it separates and divides. It is on this condition that the succession or sequence becomes a series . . . The interval is set free, the interstice becomes irreducible and stands on its own. (Deleuze 1989: 277)

The technique of cutting, which Deleuze finds equally in mathematics and film, can perfectly be used to describe his own method of bringing together different heterogeneous theories and concepts.[24]

In this article we have gathered the different heterogeneous elements, from which Deleuze's third synthesis of time emerges. Starting with Kant, it was shown how he revolutionises the philosophy of time, first, by reversing the subordination of time to movement and uncoiling the cycle of time into a straight line; second, by introducing a fracture in the I through the form of time as a form of auto-affection. Deleuze adduces Hölderlin's interpretation of Oedipus to illustrate the impact that the condition of pure and empty time has on the subject. He also gains from Hölderlin the notion of the 'caesura', which distributes a past and a future that are non-coincident or non-symmetrical. The notion of caesura finds its mathematical expression in the notion of the cut, deployed by Dedekind in order to constitute a static and purely ideal conception of continuity. Deleuze, it was argued, makes use of Dedekind's notion of a static continuum in order to create a new notion of time, which has nothing to do with the empirical phenomenon of a continuous flux of moments, but on the contrary with the notion of an a priori static synthesis, which brings together divergent series of past and present moments and future becomings. The Kantian empty form of time, which never changes, thus becomes a static synthesis of time constituted by an irrational cut. For Deleuze, the irrational cut indicates an intensive depth, an outside or virtual event, which breaks with the empirical continuation of space and time. The primary example of such a virtual event is the death of God, which Nietzsche intrinsically connects with a dissolved self. Deleuze argues that Nietzsche's eternal return is Kantianism carried to its highest and most radical form. The Kantian empty form of time produced the split subject or empirico-transcendental doublet, but Kant lost the schizophrenic momentum and reintroduced a new synthetic identity. For this reason, Deleuze resorts to Nietzsche, who maintained the dissolved self and liberated it from the rule of identity and law altogether. Faced with the death of God, the Nietzschean subject becomes ungrounded and free to run through all its possibilities of becoming: it is the universal individual or overman.

The Nietzschean thought of the eternal return is indispensable for Deleuze's third synthesis of time, which introduces a cut or caesura into consciousness and produces the system of a dissolved self. Deleuze thus ties together the themes of the Kantian empty form of time and the Nietzschean eternal return, that is, the straight line and the wheel with its centrifugal force.

This is how the story of time ends: by undoing its too well centred natural or physical circle and forming a straight line which then, led by its own length, reconstitutes an eternally decentred circle. (Deleuze 1994: 115)

Notes

1. A substantial portion of this article also appears in Chapter 4 of my book *Conditions of Thought: Deleuze and Transcendental Ideas* (Edinburgh University Press, forthcoming 2013). I gratefully acknowledge the editor's permission to republish this material.
2. See Gilles Deleuze, 'On Four Poetic Formulas which Might Summarize the Kantian Philosophy', Preface to *Kant's Critical Philosophy* (Deleuze 1984).
3. In fact, Deleuze contracts here two quotations by Rimbaud from different letters. In his letter to Georges Izambard from 13 May 1871, Rimbaud says: 'Je est un autre. Tant pis pour le bois qui se trouve violon' (Rimbaud 1975: 113), and in his letter to Paul Demeny from 15 May 1871: 'Car Je est un autre. Si le cuivre s'éveille clairon, il n'y a rien de sa faute' (Rimbaud 1975: 135).
4. See Borges 1962: 86–7.
5. Hölderlin's *Oedipus* raises the following problem: if Sophoclean tragedy already involves a thinking of the pure and empty form of time, of a time of abandonment by the gods, then the Kantian revolution, that is, the breaking with ancient cyclical time and the unrolling of time as a straight line, had already been performed in Greece two thousand years before Kant. This view fits well with Deleuze's thought that Ideas are virtual and that they become actualised in different places at different times. We should therefore read Deleuze's claim that Kant revolutionised the ancient cyclical model of time not simply in chronological terms, that is, in terms of historical development, but as the actualisation of a virtual Idea, which is to say that the movement is not going from one actual term to another, but from the virtual to the actual. We owe this suggestion to Nick Midgley.
6. See also Kant 1998: A144/B183 and A182/B224–5.
7. In this lecture course on Kant, Deleuze uses the term 'limit' in two different senses: in a first sense, limit means 'limitation' and refers to the ancient cyclical conception of time according to which time limits something, that is, measures the movements of celestial bodies. Limit in a second sense is said to be characteristic for the linear conception of time, time as pure and empty form. According to Deleuze, limit designates an internal limit, which he describes as 'that towards which something tends'. This definition matches with the mathematical definition of limit during the early geometrical phase of infinitesimal analysis, which depended upon theorems stating the continuous and infinite approximation of magnitudes toward a limiting value (Deleuze 1978b).
8. In his recently published book on Deleuze's philosophy of time, James Williams also renders 'caesura' as 'cut'. However, he does not refer to the mathematical definition of 'cut', which would have helped him in answering the question why the third synthesis is said to involve 'a formal cut, when in fact it is deduced from a somewhat narrow dramatic event (the appearance of a ghost to the Prince of Denmark)' (Williams 2011: 89).
9. It should be noted that both the rational numbers and the real numbers are infinite, ordered and dense number systems. The property of denseness means that between any two numbers there is at least one other number. Denseness is not continuity, as Bolzano mistakenly believed. The property of continuity,

which is attributed to the system of real numbers (but not to that of rational numbers), is precisely defined by Dedekind's method of cuts (see Kline 1972: 985).

10. I am indebted to Nathan Widder for drawing my attention to Russell's and Wittgenstein's critical remarks. For a comprehensive view of the mathematical debate on continuity, see Widder 2008: ch. 2, 'Point, Line, Curve', pp. 22–33.

11. For Russell, 'segments' are series of rational numbers whose terms become closer as the series progresses in order of magnitude. He defines real numbers as segments, and distinguishes segments that have limits and segments that do not (Russell 1919: 72). A rational real number, then, is defined as a segment whose terms converge to a rational limit (for instance, the series 0.49, 0.499, 0.4999,... converges to the rational number 0.5), while an irrational number is defined as a segment without limit (this shows that Russell still refers to the place of irrationals as 'gaps'). A fuller treatment of real numbers can be found in Russell 1903: chs 33 and 34. For a brief summary see Widder 2008: 27–9.

12. We do not claim that Deleuze refers to Russell or Wittgenstein; in fact, it is doubtful that Deleuze might have even known their criticism of Dedekind. But as will become clear, Russell's and, in particular, Wittgenstein's critical remarks are in a way quite close to Deleuze's modified interpretation of Dedekind.

13. By assigning to irrationals the characteristic of limits of convergent series of rational numbers, Deleuze seems to borrow from Dedekind's definition of irrationals as limits and the axiom that every series of rationals *must* have a limit – in Russell's words, Dedekind's postulation that an irrational limit had to fill the Dedekindian gap (Russell 1919: 71).

14. These two positions are not so much apart as they might seem: thinkers, such as the eighteenth-century philosopher Salomon Maimon and the Neo-Kantian philosopher Hermann Cohen, conceived differentials as both intensive magnitudes and intelligible laws of production.

15. Thus, James Williams rightly insists that Deleuze's model for the third synthesis of time cannot be the ordered line of time, and that the division produced by the caesura does not equal a thin logical point. In his own words: 'the caesura is an event and has a depth to it. It is not instantaneous but rather must be considered with its effect on the points before and after it. This is why the caesura implies a drama: it divides time such that a drama is required to encompass this division. This event-like and dramatic division is in contrast with the thin logical point and set account of the line of time where an arbitrary point is taken on a line and every point before it is defined as before in time and every point after as after in time.... This misses the process at work on Deleuze's thought and model.' (Williams 2011: 91).

It is true that Deleuze's third synthesis of time cannot be reduced to the number line and the cut to a thin logical point. But it should come as no surprise that Deleuze makes use of Dedekind's idea of a 'cut' and 'static synthesis' without following him in everything he says. Deleuze certainly over-interprets the notion of cut, insofar as he equals it with the irruption of the virtual event (the unthought, the inexplicable, the incommensurable) and the fracture in the subject.

16. For instance, in his cinema book on the time-image, Deleuze explicitly connects Borges's 'labyrinth of time' with the Nietzschean eternal return, as both conceptions of time plunge into a depth that poses 'the simultaneity of incompossible presents, or the coexistence of not-necessarily true pasts' (Deleuze 1989: 131). Borges as well as Nietzsche substitute 'the power of the false' for the form of the true, and a line of time 'which forks and keeps on forking' (131) for the empty form of time.

17. As Nathan Widder argues, the third time-image is distinctly Nietzschean, insofar as it concerns the *series of time*, while the other two time-images, which Deleuze analyses, emphasise the simultaneous layers of time and the coexistence of relations, and are thus rather Bergsonian by nature (see Widder 2008: 48–9). However, all three time-images refer to virtual time and hence 'shatter the empirical continuation of time, the chronological succession' (Deleuze 1989: 155).

18. Suffice here the following references to Klossowski by Deleuze: Deleuze 1990: 280–301 (Appendix III); 1994: 66–7, 90–1, 95, 312, 331.

19. See for instance Deleuze 1994: 6, 241–3, 299.

20. See Nietzsche 1980: 505, 11[163]: 'My doctrine teaches: live in such a way that you must desire to live again, this is your duty – you will live again in any case! He for whom striving procures the highest feeling, let him strive; he for whom repose procures the highest feeling, let him rest; he for whom belonging, following, and obeying procures the highest feeling, let him obey. Provided that he becomes aware of what procures the highest feeling, and that he shrinks back from nothing. Eternity depends upon it.'

21. See Nietzsche's letter to Jacob Burckhardt, 6 January 1889 (Nietzsche 1969: 1351).

22. See Nietzsche's letters to Peter Gast, Georg Brandes and Jacob Burckhardt from Turin, 4 January 1889 (Nietzsche 1969: 1350).

23. Michel Foucault analysed the practice of *parrhesia* in six lectures given at the University of California at Berkeley in 1983 as part of his seminar entitled 'Discourse and Truth'. The complete text compiled from tape-recordings is published under the title *Fearless Speech*, ed. Joseph Pearson, Los Angeles: Semiotext(e), 2001.

24. I am indebted to Anne Sauvagnargues for pointing out this specific Deleuzian procedure of 'cutting theories together'.

References

Aristotle (1995) *On the Heavens I & II*, ed. and trans. Stuart Leggatt, Warminster: Aris and Philips.

Borges, Jorge Luis (1962) 'Death and the Compass', in Donald A. Yates and James E. Irby (eds), *Labyrinths: Selected Stories and Other Writings*, New York: New Directions Publishing, pp. 76–87.

Boyer, Carl B. (1949) *The History of the Calculus and its Conceptual Development*, New York: Dover Publications.

Bunn, Robert (1980) 'Developments in the Foundations of Mathematics, 1870–1910', in Ivor Grattan-Guinness (ed.), *From the Calculus to Set Theory, 1630–1919: An Introductory History*, London: Duckworth, pp. 220–55.

Dedekind, Richard (1901a) 'Continuity and Irrational Numbers' (1872), in *Essays on the Theory of Numbers*, trans. Wooster Woodruff Beman, Chicago: Open Court Publishing, pp. 1–30.

Dedekind, Richard (1901b) 'The Nature and Meaning of Numbers' (1888), in *Essays on the Theory of Numbers*, trans. Wooster Woodruff Beman, Chicago: Open Court Publishing, pp. 31–115.

Deleuze, Gilles (1978a) 'Kant – 14/03/1978', trans. Melissa McMahon, available at <http://www.webdeleuze.com/php/texte.php?cle=66&groupe=Kant&langue=2> (accessed 27 August 2012).

Deleuze, Gilles (1978b) 'Kant – 21/03/1978', trans. Melissa McMahon, available at <http://www.webdeleuze.com/php/texte.php?cle=67&groupe=Kant&langue=2> (accessed 27 August 2012).

Deleuze, Gilles (1984) *Kant's Critical Philosophy*, trans. Hugh Tomlinson and Barbara Habberjam, London: Athlone Press.

Deleuze, Gilles (1989) *Cinema 2: The Time-Image*, trans. Hugh Tomlinson and Robert Galeta, London: Athlone Press.

Deleuze, Gilles (1990) *The Logic of Sense*, ed. Constantin V. Boundas, trans. Mark Lester with Charles Stivale, New York: Columbia University Press.

Deleuze, Gilles (1993) *The Fold: Leibniz and the Baroque*, trans. Tom Conley, Minneapolis: University of Minnesota Press.

Deleuze, Gilles (1994) *Difference and Repetition*, trans. Paul Patton, New York: Columbia University Press.

Deleuze, Gilles (2004) 'Conclusions on the Will to Power and the Eternal Return', in David Lapoujade (ed.), *Desert Islands and Other Texts (1953–74)*, trans. Michael Taormina, New York: Semiotext(e), pp. 117–27.

Grosz, Elizabeth (2004) *The Nick of Time: Politics, Evolution, and the Untimely*, Durham, NC and London: Duke University Press.

Hölderlin, Friedrich (1969) 'Anmerkungen zum Oedipus', in Friedrich Beißner and Jochen Schmidt (eds), *Hölderlin: Werke und Briefe*, vol. 2, Frankfurt am Main: Insel Verlag, pp. 729–36 (translations are mine).

Kant, Immanuel (1998) *Critique of Pure Reason*, ed. and trans. Paul Guyer and Allen W. Wood, Cambridge: Cambridge University Press.

Kline, Morris (1972) *Mathematical Thought from Ancient to Modern Times*, New York and Oxford: Oxford University Press.

Klossowski, Pierre (1963) 'Nietzsche, le Polythéisme et la Parodie', in *Un si funeste désir*, Paris: Gallimard, pp. 185–228.

Klossowski, Pierre (1997) 'The Experience of the Eternal Return', in *Nietzsche and the Vicious Circle*, trans. Daniel W. Smith, Chicago: University of Chicago Press, pp. 55–73.

Nietzsche, Friedrich [1917] (1936) *Thus Spake Zarathustra*, ed. Manuel Komroff, New York: Tudor.

Nietzsche, Friedrich (1969) *Briefe: 1861–1889*, in Karl Schlechta (ed.), *Werke*, vol. 3, Munich: Hanser, pp. 927–1352 (translations are mine).

Nietzsche, Friedrich (1980) *Nachgelassene Fragmente: 1880–1882*, in Giorgio Colli and Mazzino Montinari (eds), *Kritische Studienausgabe (KSA)*, vol. 9, Munich: dtv and Berlin and New York: de Gruyter (translations are mine).

Plato (1997) *Timaeus*, trans. Donald J. Zeyl, in John M. Cooper (ed.), *Plato: Complete Works*, Cambridge: Hackett Publishing, pp. 1224–91.

Rimbaud, Arthur (1975) *Lettres du Voyant*, ed. Gérard Schaeffer, Geneva: Droz and Paris: Minard.

Russell, Bertrand (1919) *Introduction to Mathematical Philosophy*, London: George Allen and Unwin.

Russell, Bertrand [1903] (1937) *The Principles of Mathematics*, 2nd edn, New York: W. W. Norton.

Widder, Nathan (2008) *Reflections on Time and Politics*, University Park, PA: The Pennsylvania State University.

Williams, James (2011) *Gilles Deleuze's Philosophy of Time: A Critical Introduction and Guide*, Edinburgh: Edinburgh University Press.

Wittgenstein, Ludwig (1956) *Remarks on the Foundations of Mathematics*, ed. G. H. von Wright, R. Rhees and G. E. M. Anscombe, trans. G. E. M. Anscombe, Oxford: Basil Blackwell.

Ontology of the Diagram and Biopolitics of Philosophy. A Research Programme on Transdisciplinarity[1]

Éric Alliez   Kingston University[2]

Abstract

In this article, the diagram is used to chart the movement from Deleuze's transcendental empiricism and engagement with structuralism in the 1960s to Deleuze and Guattari's ethico-aesthetic constructivism of the 1970s and 1980s. This is shown to culminate in a biopolitical critique and decoding of philosophy, which is part of the unfolding of a transdisciplinary research programme where art is seen to come ontologically ahead of philosophy.

Keywords: diagram, biopolitics, signs, aesthetic, structuralism, transdisciplinarity

I

In the eyes of many, my title could read as a *reparation* of the mistake Deleuze supposedly made when he translated Bacon's expression 'a sort of *graph*'[3] as *diagram* (following the French translation of 'graph'), and in doing so invested the term with nothing less than a *Logic of Sensation* dealing with the *figural* conversion of painting's fundamental 'hysteria'. This was frankly laughed at by the global village of contemporary art criticism.[4] One had to be French to learnedly explain that one needed to pass from the diagram's 'asignifying traits' – whose random marks (lines-traits, colour-patches) hurled the 'optical organisation of representation' into *catastrophe*, into *chaos* – to the 'pictorial Fact' of the painting.

Deleuze Studies 7.2 (2013): 217–230
DOI: 10.3366/dls.2013.0103
© Edinburgh University Press
www.euppublishing.com/dls

In what could not fail to appear as a classic *Aufhebung*, a line was traced between, on the one hand, the symbolic-abstract coding of the figurative which substitutes for the diagram an axiomatic that is as visual as it is mental, and on the other hand, the manual outburst where the diagram abandons its 'preparatory' stage and attacks the entire painting with its line-patch, carrying the whole surface away with it in the '*all-over*' disfiguration of action painting (Deleuze 2004c: 105–8, ch. XII: 'The Diagram').

Between Kandinsky and Pollock (or Morris)

> [t]here would thus be a tempered use of the diagram, a kind of middle way in which the diagram is not reduced to the state of a code, and yet does not cover the entire painting, avoiding both the code and its scrambling... (Deleuze 2004c: 111)

If the new figuration, whereby the figural substitutes itself for the false alternative between the figurative and the abstract, must 'emerge from the diagram', we must nonetheless *step outside the diagram* so as to 'make sensation clear and precise' (Deleuze 2004c: 110). So French, is it not, this will to organise to the point of chaos in order to 'succeed in producing a more profound resemblance' (83)... Hence the necessity of *saving the contour* of the line that delimits nothing.

One could argue that if there is an incontestable classicism here, and even so in the schematisation of the three great pathways of modern art, this classicism is rigorously determined by the will to make the 'capture of forces' (a *forcibly* Nietzschean classicism) pass through a constructivist modulation. Making use of the category of synthesiser, this constructivist modulation replaces any model of expression which would hold that forces are simply *present underneath representation*, in which particular the 'matterist' exploration realised, or was the fact of, abstract expressionism.[5] What we are dealing with is a diagram functioning '*as a modulator*' of synthesis, triply freeing planes from the perspective they replace, colour from the painterliness[6] beyond which it is deployed, and the body from the organism it overflows.[7] But this would be to engage in a defence and illustration of the pictorial aesthetic of Deleuze (a position, I say in passing, which is so unlike my own that I wrote *La Pensée-Matisse (2005)*[8] in order to depart from it *completely*). On the contrary, it seems to me that it is more interesting to accept, as all the evidence suggests, that Deleuze's *Bacon* (or, better still, the *Deleuzian Bacon*) originates from strata anterior to the double-sided works co-written with Félix Guattari (*Anti-Oedipus* (1972), *A Thousand Plateaus* (1980), with *Kafka: Toward a Minor Literature* (1975) functioning as a component of passage from one to the other).[9] In fact, the double negotiation which Deleuze's *Bacon* engages in with, on the one hand, phenomenology, and on the other hand, modernism, and which leads them to their respective points of rupture (Body without organs vs. lived body, haptic vs. optic[10]) by means of a 'diagrammatic line' held in place by the 'artistic will' (*Kunstwollen*) specific to the *aesthetic image*, testifies to this anteriority and to this independence. This is because Guattari's was a specifically *semio-political* investment in the diagram which manifested itself as the 'power of machinic assemblage [*puissance d'agencement machinique*]' (Guattari 1977: 244)[11] capable of intensely fuelling their joint work.[12]

Well before the diagram underwent its most important conceptual developments in *A Thousand Plateaus* (2004),[13] it is indeed Guattari who had already oriented Deleuze back to the term 'diagram' in an essay from 1975 on *Discipline and Punish*.[14] In this essay Deleuze focuses on the *hapax* Foucault had used when qualifying the Panopticon as 'the diagram of a mechanism of power reduced to its ideal form' (Foucault 1979: 207). But the 'ideal form' is expunged by Deleuze, who immediately connects this to a 'functioning abstracted from any obstacle, resistance or friction' (Deleuze 1975: 1216–17), allowing him to conclude that the diagram must be detached from any 'specific use', that is to say *immanent*. This immanence of the diagram involves the question of politics in an 'abstract machine... coextensive with the entire social field' (1216–17),[15] where the *pure mutations animating the diagram* must be explained by cartography. From the non-representational nature of the diagram, Deleuze in fact deduces that

> the diagram cannot be used to represent an objectivised world; on the contrary it organises a new type of reality.... The diagram is not a science, it is always a matter of politics. It is not a subject of history, nor does it survey history from above. It makes history by unmaking its previous realities and significations, constituting so many cutting edges of emergence or of creationism, of unexpected conjunctions, of improbable continua. (Deleuze 1975: 1223; my emphasis)[16]

Here the Deleuzian demonstration suddenly accelerates when it addresses the movement from one society to another through mutations of the diagram, this 'complex' problem which had, with Guattari's help, *practically* set in motion Deleuze's break with structuralism.[17] Everything here goes so quickly, one is swept away by phrases manifesting the *diagrammatic forcing* of the Foucauldian concept of apparatus of power, that really one must project oneself several years forwards, to *A Thousand Plateaus*, where the differences now established between Deleuze–Guattari (or Guattari–Deleuze[18]) and Foucault are made explicit, to be able to understand the reasons for these differences. One must adopt the perspective of this 'new way of thinking' which is no longer just 'diagrammatism' (as Deleuze put it in his article from 1975[19]) but *a new way of thinking about the diagram affirmed in its full machinic alterity*: 'the diagram and abstract machine have lines of flight that are primary, which are not phenomena of resistance or counterattack in an assemblage, but cutting edges of creation and deterritorialisation' (Deleuze and Guattari 2004: 585, n.39). Assemblages will thus no longer be 'of power but of desire (desire is always assembled), and power seems to be a stratified dimension of the assemblage'[20] (585, n.39). It is at the end of this Copernican Revolution in desire/power, which involves an entire constructivism of desire dependent on its complete immanence to the social field, that the machine-diagram will be called *abstract insofar as it 'constitutes and conjugates all of the assemblage's cutting edges of deterritorialisation'* (155). So much so that the *enforced* deterritorialisation of the diagram comes first, as the *machinic* key to the movement from the dimension of historical formations as strata to the non-stratified dimension of power as strategy, as found in *Discipline and Punish*. From the archive to the diagram . . . or from the History (of forms) to the becoming (of forces). We must understand here *a becoming capable of explaining the prevalence of relations of power over relations of knowledge without, nonetheless, remaining imprisoned by 'the immanence of power'*.

(Foucault will himself take on this problem in *The History of Sexuality: The Will to Knowledge*, independently of the *biopolitical critique of philosophy* which it implies for Deleuze *with Guattari*:

> Should it be said that one is always 'inside' power, there is no 'escaping' it, there is no absolute outside where it is concerned, because one is subject to the law in any case? Or that, history being the ruse of reason, power is the ruse of history, always emerging the winner? (Foucault 1998: 95)[21])

Since Deleuze credits Foucault with the notion of 'assemblage' (*agencement*) in his article from 1975,[22] it is therefore at the level of this reoriented 'assemblage' that the Foucauldian problematic of power-knowledge will be renewed, as well as its later adjustment in terms of the relation between discursive formations (referring to the sayable, the set of all enunciations) and non-discursive formations (which designate, in its positive sense (*dans sa forme positive*), the visible, the set of all bodies). In this relation between formations one must bear in mind that it is necessary to affirm both their *de jure* heterogeneity and *de facto* interpenetration, which are irreducible to the pairing between signifier and signified.[23] Deleuze renewed this in terms (alien to Foucault) of *form of expression* (the sayable) and *form of content* (the visible),[24] which are put in relation and in *relations of force* in a double-sided assemblage which does not formalise expression as an 'assemblage of enunciation' without also formalising contents as a 'machinic assemblage, or an assemblage of bodies' (Deleuze and Guattari 2004: 155). Deleuze and Guattari go on to say that

> [w]e must therefore arrive at something in the assemblage itself that is still more profound than these sides and can account for both of the forms in presupposition, forms of expression or regimes of signs (semiotic systems) and forms of content or regimes of bodies (physical systems). (Deleuze and Guattari 2004: 155)

And it is thanks to Guattari's semiotics and pragmatic critique of linguistics, inspired by a *de-structuralised* Hjelmslev,[25] that the concepts of abstract machine and diagram will inter-define this 'something ... that is still more profound' (Deleuze and Guattari 2004: 155) where there is no longer either any substance or form, content or expression, but *'traits' of content and of expression* functioning to ensure the most deterritorialised of connections between '*pure matter*', that is, unformed matters or *intensities*, and '*pure function*', that is, informal functions or '*tensors*' (156).[26] At the level of 'the most deterritorialised content and [of] the most deterritorialised expression' (156), retained by the diagram 'in order to conjugate them' (156), one can thus recognise the etymo-archaeology of the diagram as a drawing-writing. Binding itself to (*en prise sur*) a becoming of forces-signs which are at work in the strata, the diagram is the surface of experimentation of an Abstract-Real (*un Abstrait-Réel*), of a writing *flush with the real writing a new type of reality* held in the very fabric of the most concrete of assemblages by the joint deterritorialisation of expression and content. We are dealing with the *virtualities* of a 'revolutionary diagram from which are derived both a new way of doing and a new way of speaking' (Deleuze 1975: 1227) in conditions that will 'display the relations of force constitutive of power' (1227) – and that will reveal economic materialism[27] to be the other side of the structuralist idealism of the signifier – in order to diagram the informal element of forces in which both the visible and the sayable are submerged. It is in these relations of force *between content and expression* that, on the one hand, 'the stabilisation of relations of deterritorialisation' (Guattari 1977: 243) determines itself from the viewpoint of power and, on the other hand, that is assembled an intensive deterritorialising machine carried by the flows of signs which it involves in diagrammatic processes of conjunction, which are always more dominant over the material flows of all kinds and in which they are at work *anyway*.

It is now my turn to accelerate, and to say all too quickly that we do not touch on the diagrammatic *implication* of Deleuzo-Guattarian (and/or Guattaro-Deleuzian) thought in its most political plane of consistency without it immediately *explicating* and complicating itself as *Art and Politics*. For even if art cannot bring to light the most contemporary 'capture of forces' without also *harnessing the intense-abstract light of the diagram* – 'which renders the sayable visible, and which renders action sayable – but for another language, for another way of acting' (Deleuze 1975: 1226) – the social field must nonetheless first define itself by its lines of flight so that the conjunction (in art *and* politics) can *construct a real to come*. This is a 'Real-Abstract [which] opposes itself all the more to the fictitious abstraction of a supposedly pure machine of expression' (Deleuze and Guattari 2004: 157; translation modified) since it tries to *bring about the continuum, the conjunction of all that flees (tout ce qui fuit) and of everything that slides under – and pushes through – the grid or net*. Or to put it another way: so that art ceases to be an end in itself, the artist must – in one way or another, but in the most singular of ways – invest him- or herself in this 'social' affirmation by experimenting with 'signs', not as bearers of *something else* (the invisible at work in the visual-aesthetic image), but as *forces-signs of deterritorialisation and of reterritorialisation*. So art is never an end in itself,

> it is only a tool for blazing life lines, in other words, all of those real becomings that are not produced only *in* art, and all of those active escapes that do not consist in fleeing *into* art, taking refuge in art, and all of those positive deterritorialisations that never reterritorialise on art, but instead sweep it away with them toward the realms of the asignifying, asubjective, and faceless. (Deleuze and Guattari 2004: 208)

It is this *sign-aisthesic*[28] (*signesthésique*) politics of art which can be called, as a rigorous contemporary alternative to its 'conceptual' version, *Art after Philosophy*. This 'after' (*après*) does not mean art '*according to*' (*d'après*) philosophy – nor does it mean an analytical finish or varnish (*un apprêt*) applied to philosophy (à la Kosuth) – since ontologically art comes *ahead of* it (*en-avant*) (along with the *postconceptual* critique/clinique of philosophy which it carries with it).

II

To develop this political ontology of the diagram into a biopolitical critique of philosophy and to envelop in its plane of immanence the construction of the question of transdisciplinarity – *as postphilosophical problem* – one must first make the art–politics conjunction operate retroactively on (*rabattre sur*) the historico-philosophical sequence which *stretched the former between Deleuze and Guattari*. In one direction we will find this constitutive affirmation of transcendental empiricism in the *Difference and Repetition of philosophy*, where it is the role of 'the modern work of art' to indicate 'to philosophy a path which leads to the abandonment of representation' by identifying the conditions of real experience – instead of and replacing the conditions of possible experience – (the) experimentation in and of the work of art (*l'expérimentation de/dans l'œuvre d'art*), with the development of its simulacral 'permutating series' (Deleuze 1994: 65–8), etc. This is thus one path, a post/structuralist logic of sense. In the other direction we will be taken to 'this ontological root of creativity that is characteristic of the new processual paradigm' (Guattari 1995: 116), which Guattari preferred to call the 'proto-aesthetic [rather than 'aesthetic'] paradigm' (101), 'to emphasise that we are not referring to institutionalised art' (102), and that the two (Kantian) meanings of aesthetic (theory of the sensible and theory of the beautiful) would be less *conflated in the work of art*[29] than they would be *absolutely deterritorialised* in the 'machination for producing existence' (109), in the 'generative praxis [of] heterogeneity and complexity' (109). We know that such praxis involves this '*diagrammatic politics*' (Guattari 2011: 174), its equally semiotic and material 'onto-logic'[30] having been thoroughly explored in *A Thousand Plateaus* as a machinic and critical (*machinique-critique*) alternative to the play of series on the surface of structures. But it is inevitably also an alternative to the philosophical re-foundation of the transdisciplinary research programme initiated by structuralism, a structuralism which Deleuze had reworked as a 'new transcendental philosophy' (Deleuze 2004a: 174), before giving in to the *anti-structuralist motif* developed in 'real time' (the paradigmatic axis) by Guattari[31] since the *anti-Oedipus* could equally well read as *anti-structure*.[32] Here we must weave (*croiser*) our first historico-philosophical sequence into a second, reorienting the question of transdisciplinarity as *problem of philosophy*.

This sequence starts with the transdisciplinary research programme of structuralism based on linguistics' structural functionalism and developed in a transformative system of relations mobilising the humanities and social sciences *against the theoretical primacy of philosophy*. This first 'moment' is followed by a *philosophical re-foundation of transdisciplinarity* through the re-definition of structuralism as *the* 'new transcendental philosophy' (Deleuze 2004a: 174), Deleuze's key expression in 'How do We Recognize Structuralism?' – and let us notice (1) that it tends to a *poststructuralist complication* of Structuralism's problematics by a full integration or transduction of Deleuzian 'superior empiricism' (Deleuze's post-Bergsonian *bio-transcendental* empiricism is *differentially re-actualised* in post/structuralist terms); (2) and that, at the end of the article (written in 1967, that is, contemporary with the *Structuralist Controversy*, the Baltimore Conference), Deleuze reinvests or reworks, with the question of the 'structural mutations', the structure/genesis or system/transformation problem in practical terms which are understood as a *challenge to (the new transcendental) philosophy* and as *the criteria of the future*. The third moment – but the transdisciplinary problematics oblige us to reunify *in tension* the three moments – is the moment of the 'rhizome' as this anti-structuralist war machine that can only make *structure take flight* (according to a machinic apparatus that appropriates structure's real-abstraction so as to *animate the whole process radically put into becoming from the outside*) by producing a critique/clinique of philosophy, a kind of *schizoanalysis of philosophy* undertaken from the radical perspective of a *politics of transversalisation* liberating transdisciplinarity from its structural *ordination* as *disciplinary regulation* of structuralist transdisciplinarity (the operational closure of the structure). At the end of the day, Lévi-Straussian *bricolage* is substituted for a pragmatics starting to work as a critical developer of the political economy of language. Pragmatics means thus an anti-linguistic ontology of the sign that extracts the transformational component of post-structuralism, that is, *structuralism driven to its constitutive tension*, redirecting it diagrammatically towards *a total de-epistemologisation and re-ontologisation* to attain – 'at the absolute horizon of all processes of creation': which is to say an 'ontological transversality' (Guattari 1995: 38) – a *politics of multiplicities* as a *postphilosophical ungrounding (effondement)* of transdisciplinarity. At its point of greatest tension, in a *post modo*[33] modality which is none other than the politics of thought and politics inside thought (*la politique de/dans la pensée*), as oriented by the analysis of capitalism, it reads, as Guattari puts it: 'Being does not precede machinic essence; the process precedes the heterogenesis of being' (108).

What is at stake in this rupture is a renewed machinic biopolitics of 'assemblages'. The rupture will have begun by *opposing* transdisciplinary experimentation to 'structural interpretation' at the same moment that the 'critique of philosophy' exceeds the philosophy of representation[34] to involve itself in a *clinical practice of the social sciences* (meaning a practice of *all* the human sciences, which become at once pragmatic – and de-structuralised – and political – and re-socialised). For if Guattari puts an end to the project Deleuze had long had of opening philosophy up to *artist-thought* (*la pensée-artiste*) and of *aesthetically* intensifying its system of interpretation in order to let in its own outside (which *forces* it to think, as constrained by the sensibility and the real conditions of these 'new works of today'[35]), it is indeed because his assemblage with Guattari bears a whole new potentiality (and effect) which became necessary after 1968. That is, to make philosophy step outside itself by undergoing a process of *decoding*, which functions textually and arrives at its logic of sense *at the same time* that this process invests the destruction of the codes used by capitalism to represent this very process, and in a historical narrative inseparable from a *semiotic machination* of the subject. (It is here that *Foucault-thought* (*la pensée-Foucault*) will be invested with a *diagrammatic function*.) This means that Deleuze will put the Guattari-effect to work in a biopolitical critique of philosophy which, brought outside itself and into the social field, gains an absolute power of decoding. Its *first effect* will be to undo the philosophical image of thought by breaking that which codes its material-ideal form of interiority. This is the 'book of philosophy' which we no longer propose to replace with another form of *expression* and a new *style* – as Deleuze famously puts it in the preface to *Difference and Repetition*: 'The time is coming when it will hardly be possible to write a book of philosophy as it has been done for so long: "Ah! the old style . . . "' (Deleuze 1994: xxi). Instead, we oppose to it another regime of production which *incorporates* the 'book of philosophy' into the material *milieu* by *plugging* it into the *machinic* conditions of reality of the most external and the most internal of forces. The diagram names this process where signs flush with material flows[36] – and whose cutting edges of creation are ontologically affirmed and analytically assisted – turn back on philosophy's reterritorialisation onto the concept, at the very same moment that philosophy absolutely deterritorialises capital (*porte à l'absolu la déterritorialisation relative du capital*) by suppressing it as an internal limit (Deleuze and Guattari 2003: 98). Postconceptual or postphilosophical mean nothing else than the following: that the general function of diagrammatisation proliferates beyond itself; not 'in general' – either *philosophically* in general or generally in a *philosophical* manner, solely because of the identity-alterity (not so recently) posited BEING = BECOMING, or MONISM = PLURALISM, 'the furniture we are forever rearranging' (Deleuze and Guattari 2004: 23) – but rather in *an* assemblage *to be constructed*, always as both a 'collective assemblage of enunciation' and a 'machinic assemblage of desire'.[37]

Notes

1. This paper was presented at the 'Deleuze, Philosophy, Transdisciplinarity' Conference, Goldsmiths University of London, 10–12 February 2012, and is part of the CRMEP's research programme on Transdisciplinarity (AHRC 914469, with P. Osborne and S. Stanford). With the exception of the endnotes, no major changes have been introduced for this publication. When referencing in dual languages, non-English editions of texts follow the English language references.
2. Translated by Guillaume Collett.
3. As found in his Interviews with David Sylvester: *The Brutality of Fact: Interviews with Francis Bacon* (Sylvester 1975: 56/110–11).
4. Cf. Art & Language, T. Baldwin 2004; Roberts 2010 – the first lines of the article read: 'Modern continental philosophers – or more precisely modern French philosophers – have, historically, not been the best or most welcome judges of art. When they have not been hitching a ride on the back of some blue chip reputation in order to stoke the fires of high-end conceptualisation, they have been scuttling around in artistic marginalia pursuing some unfathomable fancy, like a love-struck teenager indifferent to the absurdity of their love-object. Top prize in the former category goes to Deleuze's hystericised Francis Bacon as grand master . . .' (Roberts 2010: 70).
5. 'But with Pollock, this line-trait and this colour-patch will be pushed to their functional limit . . . a decomposition of matter, which abandons us to its lineaments and granulations' (Deleuze 2004c: 105). Matterism here would be the fruit of the diagram's own self-reflexivity: 'rather than making the flux pass through the diagram . . . , it is as if the diagram were directed toward itself' (117). Matterism *qua* Mannerism.
6. [Translator's note: this is the standard translation of the German *malerisch*, used by Alliez, a word popularised by Swiss art historian Heinrich Wölfflin (1864–1945). This term refers to a manner of painting in a less than controlled style, where the brushstrokes themselves are visible or spill over the drawn lines. Painterliness is found particularly in impressionism and abstract expressionism.]
7. See the whole of Deleuze [1969] 2004b: ch. XIII, 'Analogy'
8. A recent development from this work has been published; see Alliez 2012.
9. Published in 1981, which is to say one year after *A Thousand Plateaus*, *Francis Bacon: The Logic of Sensation* (2004c) can be considered as directly and autonomously related to *The Logic of Sense* (2004b), *short-circuited* by the hysteria of Artaud's Body without Organs, which endows sensation with a radically non-phenomenological logic (cf. 2004c: ch. VII: 'Hysteria'). The volcanic eruption of the Body without Organs in the very middle of the structuralist logic of sense (13th series) in truth had already put an end to this philosophical project for Deleuze himself.

10. But haptic could equally lead, via Hildebrand, to a modernist phenomenology of art.
11. If it is too late not to follow the standard translation of '*agencement*' as 'assemblage', we ask the reader to keep in mind the '*agencement*' as a *diagrammatic kind of agency.*
12. Cf. Guattari 1977, 1979, 2006, 2011.
13. Developments of the diagram are indissociable from a pragmatics of signs of which we will find more than one sketch in Félix Guattari's *The Machinic Unconscious* (2011), first published in 1979 before *A Thousand Plateaus.*
14. 'Écrivain non: un nouveau cartographe' (Deleuze 1975). The article is republished in a very modified form in *Foucault* under the general title of 'From the Archive to the Diagram' (2006: 1–38).
15. For the Guattarian heterogenesis of the concept of 'abstract machine', see for example Guattari 1995: 35.
16. 'It doubles history with a sense of continual evolution [or becoming]', concludes Deleuze when he repeats this phrase in *Foucault* (2006: 31) (translation modified).
17. It is the end of the article entitled 'How Do We Recognise Structuralism?' (Deleuze 2004a: 170–192) where Deleuze must launch a 'structuralist hero' so as to set up a praxis there.
18. For the montage of this syntagm, cf. Alliez 2011.
19. 'Une nouvelle pensée, positive et positiviste, *le diagrammatisme, la cartographie*' (Deleuze 1975: 1223; original emphasis).
20. See Deleuze 2007: we will find the differential principle of the Deleuzo-Guattarian note on Foucault of *A Thousand Plateaus* in this letter addressed to Foucault after *The History of Sexuality: The Will to Knowledge* was published in 1976.
21. Profoundly different from the Deleuzo-Guattarian 'lines of flight', Foucault's political philosophy requires a notion of 'resistance', considered as irreducible vis-à-vis relations of power.
22. Resolutely Deleuzo-Guattarian (and not Foucauldian), the concept of assemblage appears for the first time in *Kafka: Toward a Minor Literature* (1986), particularly in the last chapter ('What is an Assemblage?/Qu'est-ce qu'un agencement?').
23. In *A Thousand Plateaus* (2004: 66), Deleuze and Guattari return to the whole analysis of the diagram-prison (which makes them return to *The Archaeology of Knowledge*).
24. Cf. Deleuze 1975: 1213, 1219ff. These two terms come from the Danish linguist Hjelmslev from whom Guattari had long appropriated this distinction – not without modifying its structuralist character in order to radicalise the rupture with the pairing between signifier and signified. Cf. Hjelmslev 1968, particularly ch. 13 cited in *A Thousand Plateaus.*
25. Since form continues to fall on matter 'like a net' (an expression of Hjelmslev's) to engender substance as much of expression as of content. Cf. Guattari 1995: 24, 1979: 226.
26. Cf. Deleuze 1975: 1216–17, for the first appearance of the analysis of diagrammatism developed in terms of 'pure function' and 'pure matter' – and related to the Panopticon insofar as it ignores the finalisation of functions (caring for or supervising (*surveiller*), teaching or punishing, etc.), and the organisation of matters (hospital or workshop, school or prison, etc.), from which is derived its 'informal' dimension.
27. 'In any case, content and expression are never reducible to signified-signifier. And ... neither are they reducible to base-superstructure. One can no more posit

a primacy of content as the determining factor than a primacy of expression as a signifying system' (Deleuze and Guattari 2004: 76). The lesson here is as much Foucauldian as it is Guattarian (Guattari's anti-Althusserianism).

28. [Translator's note: the Greek term *aisthesis* (αισθησις) refers to sensation, perception, as opposed to intellection (*noesis*). Alberto Toscano explains that, following Alliez's 'distinctive concern with the sensible conditions of philosophy, science and art', *aisthesis* functions 'transversal[ly] ... as both affect and experiment, passive synthesis and invention'; see Toscano's preface to Alliez 2004: xi. We should hear echoes of a transversal or transdisciplinary 'synaesthesia' (*synesthésie*) in Alliez's neologism.]

29. Cf. Deleuze (1994: 82): 'Everything changes once we determine the conditions of real experience, which are not larger than the conditioned and which differ in kind from the categories: the two senses of the aesthetic become one, to the point where the being of the sensible reveals itself in the work of art, while at the same time the work of art appears as experimentation.'

30. This is another term Guattari uses; cf. Guattari 1995: 65.

31. See the texts collected in Guattari 1972 – with a preface by Deleuze.

32. Following – and *as an inversion of* – J.-C. Milner's expression in *Le Périple structural* (2002).

33. [Translator's note: in *The Postmodern Condition: A Report on Knowledge*, J.-F. Lyotard tells us that '*Post modern* would have to be understood according to the paradox of the future (*post*) anterior (*modo*)' (1984: 81).]

34. According to the movement of thought which leads Deleuze from the Nietzschean critique of Kant to an anti-representative philosophy of Difference and Repetition at first commanded by the post-Romantic appropriation of Proustian literary experience. It is here that 'Thereby is manifested the "philosophical" bearing of Proust's work: it vies with philosophy' (Deleuze 2000: 94), while art is the exclusive domain of an experimentation whose 'problematic' character is precisely defined by its interpretation. This will be reproblematised in structuralist terms ('structural interpretation' in fact comes from the *first* criterion by which we recognise structuralism: the symbolic; cf. Deleuze, 'How do We Recognise Structuralism?', *op. cit.*, p. 172).

35. As 'this [structural] reinterpretation only has value to the extent that it animates new works which are those of today' (Deleuze 2004a: 173). This is the key example of Pop Art in *Difference and Repetition*.

36. According to the animation stands of 'Échafaudages sémiotiques' (1977: 250ff.).

37. This is the definition of assemblage proposed by Deleuze and Guattari at the end of *Kafka: Toward a Minor Literature* (1986). This is thus rigorously contemporary with Deleuze's 'diagrammatic' article on Foucault. – To conclude in a kind of re-opening, let me say that this *paper* had no other aim than to explore this contemporary diagrammatic regime by means of the unfolding of the same gesture in which I oppose the 'aesthetic regime' of Jacques Rancière. On this diagrammatic agency vs. aesthetic regime, see my 'Body without Image: Ernesto Neto's Anti-Leviathan' (2013 forthcoming).

References

Alliez, Éric (2004) *The Signature of the World, What is Deleuze and Guattari's Philosophy?*, trans. Eliot Ross Albert and Alberto Toscano, London: Continuum.

Alliez, Éric (2012) 'Matisse in the Becoming-Architecture of Painting', in E. Whittaker and A. Landrum (eds), *Painting with Architecture in Mind*, Bath: Wunderkammer Press, pp. 38–70.

Alliez, Éric (forthcoming 2013) 'Body without Image: Ernesto Neto's Anti-Leviathan', in É. Alliez and P. Osborne (eds.), *Spheres of Action: Art and Politics*, London: Tate Publishing.

Alliez, Éric and Bonne, Jean-Claude (2005) *La Pensée-Matisse. Portrait de l'artiste en hyperfauve*, Paris: Le Passage.

Alliez, Éric (2011) 'The Guattari-Deleuze Effect', in Éric Alliez and Andrew Goffey, *The Guattari Effect*, London: Continuum, pp. 260–74.

Baldwin, Thomas (2004) 'Deleuze's Bacon', *Radical Philosophy*, 123, pp. 29–40.

Deleuze, Gilles (1975) 'Écrivain non: un nouveau cartographe', *Critique*, 343, pp. 1207–27.

Deleuze, Gilles [1968] (1994) *Difference and Repetition*, trans. Paul Patton, New York: Columbia University Press.

Deleuze, Gilles [1972, 2nd edn] (2000) *Proust and Signs*, trans. Richard Howard, London: Athlone Press.

Deleuze, Gilles (2004a) 'How Do We Recognise Structuralism?', in *Desert Islands and Other Texts, 1953–1974*, trans. Michael Taormina, London: Semiotext(e) and MIT Press, pp. 170–92.

Deleuze, Gilles [1969] (2004b) *The Logic of Sense*, trans. Mark Lester and Charles Stivale, London: Continuum.

Deleuze, Gilles [1981] (2004c) *Francis Bacon. The Logic of Sensation*, trans. Daniel W. Smith, London: Continuum.

Deleuze, Gilles [1986] (2006) *Foucault*, trans. Seán Hand, London: Continuum.

Deleuze, Gilles (2007) 'Desire and Pleasure' (1977), in *Two Regimes of Madness, Texts and Interviews 1975–1995*, trans. Ames Hodges and Mike Taormina, London: Semiotext(e) and MIT Press, pp. 122–34.

Deleuze, Gilles and Félix Guattari [1975] (1986) *Kafka: Toward a Minor Literature*, trans. Dana Polan, Minneapolis: University of Minnesota Press.

Deleuze, Gilles and Félix Guattari [1991] (2003) *What is Philosophy?*, trans. Hugh Tomlinson and Graham Burchell, London: Verso.

Deleuze, Gilles and Félix Guattari [1980] (2004) *A Thousand Plateaus: Capitalism and Schizophrenia*, trans. Brian Massumi, London: Continuum.

Foucault, Michel [1975] (1979) *Discipline and Punish*, trans. Alan Sheridan, London: Vintage Books.

Foucault, Michel [1976] (1998) *The Will to Knowledge: The History of Sexuality Volume 1*, trans. Robert Hurley, London: Penguin.

Guattari, Félix (1972) *Psychanalyse et transversalité*, Paris: Maspéro.

Guattari, Félix (1977) 'Échafaudages sémiotiques', in *La Révolution moléculaire*, Paris: Encres-Recherches, pp. 239–376.

Guattari, Félix (1979) *L'Inconscient machinique*, Paris: Encres-Recherches.

Guattari, Félix [1992] (1995) *Chaosmosis: An Ethico-aesthetic Paradigm*, trans. Paul Bains and Julian Pefanis, Bloomington and Indianapolis: Indiana University Press.

Guattari, Félix (2006) *The Anti-Oedipus Papers*, London: Semiotext(e) and MIT Press.

Guattari, Félix [1979] (2011) *The Machinic Unconscious*, trans. Taylor Adkins, London: Semiotext(e) and MIT Press.

Hjelmslev, Louis (1968) *Prolégomènes à une théorie du langage*, Paris: Éditions de Minuit.

Lyotard, Jean-François [1979] (1984) *The Postmodern Condition: A Report on Knowledge*, trans. G. Bennington and B. Massumi, University of Minnesota Press: Minneapolis.

Milner, Jean-Claude (2002) *Le Périple structural*, Paris: Seuil.

Roberts, J. (2010) 'Philosophy, culture, image: Rancière's "constructivism"', *Philosophy of Photography*, 1:1, pp. 69–81.

Sylvester, David (1975) *The Brutality of Fact: Interviews with Francis Bacon*, London: Thames and Hudson.

Sylvester, David (1976) *L'Art de l'impossible. Entretiens avec David Sylvester*, Geneva: Skira.

Who Are Our Nomads Today?: Deleuze's Political Ontology and the Revolutionary Problematic

Craig Lundy   University of Wollongong

Abstract

This paper will address the question of the revolution in Gilles Deleuze's political ontology. More specifically, it will explore what kind of person Deleuze believes is capable of bringing about genuine and practical transformation. Contrary to the belief that a Deleuzian programme for change centres on the facilitation of 'absolute deterritorialisation' and pure 'lines of flight', I will demonstrate how Deleuze in fact advocates a more cautious and incremental if not conservative practice that promotes the ethic of prudence. This will be achieved in part through a critical analysis of the dualistic premises upon which much Deleuzian political philosophy is based, alongside the topological triads that can also be found in his work. In light of this critique, Deleuze's thoughts on what it is to be and become a revolutionary will be brought into relief, giving rise to the question: who really is Deleuze's nomad, his true revolutionary or figure of transformation?

Keywords: nomads, political ontology, multiplicities, State, dualisms and triads

Introduction

In concluding a paper titled 'Nomadic Thought' delivered to a Nietzsche conference in 1972, Gilles Deleuze sums up the problem of the revolution as follows:

Deleuze Studies 7.2 (2013): 231–249
DOI: 10.3366/dls.2013.0104
© Edinburgh University Press
www.euppublishing.com/dls

As we know, the revolutionary problem today is to find some unity in our various struggles without falling back on the despotic and bureaucratic organization of the party or State apparatus: we want a war-machine that would not recreate a State apparatus, a nomadic unity in relation with the Outside, that would not recreate the despotic internal unity. (Deleuze 2004: 259)

It is no longer the early 1970s, and our world has changed significantly since then. But although the question of 'the revolution' that troubled the political Left of Deleuze's France has changed in tenor somewhat, the problem which Deleuze refers to in the above passage is arguably as pressing now as it has ever been. Recent revolutionary events across North Africa, the Middle East and Greece obviously spring to mind, as does the ongoing attempt of environmentalists to 'find some unity' for their movement, or more specifically, a mechanism that can successfully coordinate mass-action in a way that does not wait for or rely upon State apparatuses. Others are better placed than I am to comment on the particularities of these examples. What I would like to do in this paper, however, is not so much speak about the specifics of these struggles, as investigate what Deleuzian philosophy and politics have to say about revolutionaries in general. In short, who is, according to Deleuze's practice of thought, a real nomad or revolutionary? Who is it that is capable of bringing about genuine and practical transformation? Contrary to the belief that a Deleuzian programme for change centres on the facilitation of absolute deterritorialisation and pure lines of flight, I will demonstrate in this paper how Deleuze in fact advocates a more cautious and incremental if not conservative approach – an approach, moreover, that is revolutionary precisely because of its distancing from the absolute in favour of prudence.

It must be acknowledged from the outset that Deleuze will not exactly provide us with an explicit answer to the question in this paper's title. This is because instead of naming names and setting down step-by-step instructions, Deleuze directs his energies towards altering our understanding and approach to the question of who is a revolutionary and the revolutionary problematic it is a part of. Appreciating the nature of this alteration and the ontology that underpins it will therefore form the major task of this paper. It will be pursued through a close examination of the relevant primary material.[1] To begin with, I will briefly touch on some of the abiding dualisms in Deleuze's work that are largely responsible for determining the shape and direction for much of his political philosophy. Chief among these will be the dualism mentioned in the above quote of the nomad and the State. Following this initial presentation, which will evidence Deleuze's transdisciplinary practice, I will demonstrate how this basic and well-formed dualism is far more complex than it might initially seem. In fact, I will show how Deleuze's political ontology contains not one but two possible nomads, thus calling into question the dualistic premises upon which much Deleuzian commentary and Deleuzian-inspired political thought is based. After distinguishing between these two nomadic figures, the question with which Deleuze closes his 'Nomadic Thought' essay will be rejoined: who really are our nomads today, our true revolutionary figures of transformation?[2]

Absolute Nomads

1972 was a big year for Deleuze. That year saw the publication of a number of important works, including his much discussed interview with Michel Foucault 'Intellectuals and Power', and his key essay 'How Do We Recognise Structuralism?'. More significantly, it was in that year that *Anti-Oedipus* first appeared. But while there is a good chance that the participants at the 'Nietzsche Today' conference held in the summer of that year at Cerisy-la-Salle (which included luminaries such as Klossowski, Derrida, Lyotard, Nancy, Gandillac and Lacoue-Labarthe) would have been aware of Deleuze's new philosophical direction with Guattari, it is highly unlikely that they would have had any idea what exactly he was referring to in his paper by the conceptual distinction between the nomad and the State. Indeed, when asked a question by Mieke Taat in the discussion following Deleuze's paper about the incongruity between his current work and certain positions in his last book (*The Logic of Sense*), Deleuze simply responded: 'I've undergone a change' (Deleuze 2004: 261). Four years later Deleuze would elaborate on this curt (and rather unsatisfactory) response:

> Fortunately I am nearly incapable of speaking for myself, because what has happened to me since *The Logic of Sense* now depends on my having met Félix Guattari, on my work with him, on what we do together. I believe Félix and I sought out new directions simply because we felt like doing so.... I believe also that this change of method brings with it a change of subject matter, or, vice versa, that a certain kind of politics takes the place of psychoanalysis [the method of *The Logic of Sense*]. Such a method would also be a form of politics (micropolitics) and would propose the study of multiplicities... (Deleuze 2006: 65–6)

Taking advantage of this collaborative material, we find ourselves in a position denied the participants at Cerisy to make sense of Deleuze's understanding and treatment of what he referred to as 'the revolutionary problem today'. What Deleuze is after, to restate his presentation of the problematic, is a way of organising a revolutionary movement, or more specifically, revolutionary *force*, that does not end up reproducing what it is fighting against in the act of resistance. Pure anarchy is one thing, and at certain times a good thing. But such disorganisation is statedly not Deleuze's objective. For him, the question is more exactly: is there a way of *organising* that is more structured than pure anarchy yet avoids the despotic State form? This is Deleuze's revolutionary problem.[3] His response with Guattari is for the most part strategic, as befits the practical thrust of the problem. But it is also ontological. Let us then briefly look at the ontological basis for Deleuze's political philosophy, before specifically turning to his various statements on revolutionaries.[4]

In seeking an alternative kind of organisation to the State form, Deleuze and Guattari nominate its historical opponent: the nomad. It is most common for the term 'nomos' to be associated with the law. Deleuze and Guattari, however, contest this straight connotation by emphasising its opposition to the 'polis':

> The *nomos* came to designate the law, but that was originally because it was distribution, a mode of distribution. It is a very special kind of distribution, one without division into shares, in a space without borders or enclosure. The *nomos* is the consistency of a fuzzy aggregate: it is in this sense that it stands in opposition to the law or the *polis*, as the backcountry, a mountainside, or the vague expanse around a city ('either nomos or polis'). (Deleuze and Guattari 1987: 380)[5]

The nomad and the State thus form a dualism for Deleuze and Guattari, whereby the State works to 'reclaim' land by building 'walls, enclosures, and roads between enclosures' while the nomads do not so much tame the earth as populate its expanse, inserting themselves into the continually shifting nature of the desert, tundra, etc. (Deleuze and Guattari 1987: 381).

As this description suggests, the distinction between the nomad and the State is largely predicated on their differing relations to space, and more precisely, their distribution *of* and *in* space. Deleuze had been playing around with this distinction for some time. As he explains in *Difference and Repetition*, there are two types of distribution, one 'which implies a dividing up of that which is distributed' and another which is 'a division among those who distribute *themselves* in an open space – a space which is unlimited, or at least without precise limits' (Deleuze 1994: 36).[6] Moving forward to *A Thousand Plateaus*, Deleuze and Guattari discover another novel way to describe this distinction, employing terms created by the musical composer Pierre Boulez. In his musical compositions, Boulez distinguishes between a smooth space-time that 'one occupies without counting' and a striated space-time that 'one counts in order to occupy' (Deleuze and Guattari 1987: 477). These two ways of engaging with sound involve contrasting attitudes towards, and experiences of, space-time. In a striated space, a 'standard' is imposed onto music, providing an organisational structure to which sounds then correspond. Frequencies of sound are thus distributed within various intervals respective to the breaks that separate them. In a smooth space, on the other hand, frequencies are distributed without breaks; there is no transcendent scale from which to judge the frequency, for the space-time itself continuously modulates. For this reason, smooth space has no boundaries between one interval and another – there is no inside and outside – since it is composed entirely of an alteration that continuously expands or unravels.

At base, however, all of these distinctions of smooth/striated and nomad/State can be traced back to one of the earliest and most enduring of Deleuzian dualisms: Henri Bergson's separation between differences of nature and differences of degree. As Deleuze explains in his 1956 essay 'Bergson's Conception of Difference', differences of nature are heterogeneous while differences of degree are homogeneous (Deleuze 2004: 32–51). This means that for a difference of nature to be genuinely heterogeneous, it must not merely refer to the difference between two homogeneities, since this would reduce heterogeneity to the identity of homogeneities. Therefore, a difference of nature must differ first and foremost *from itself*: what defines a difference of nature is not merely the way it differs from other external objects, but the way it differs internally, being composed of a heterogeneity on the inside.

Another way that Bergson describes this separation of difference is by employing the theory of multiplicities as developed by the mathematician Bernhard Riemann. Following Riemann, Bergson distinguishes between metric and nonmetric multiplicities, or in other words, those multiplicities that can and cannot be divided without changing in kind. Metric multiplicities lend themselves to striation, for they can be easily sub-divided and manipulated without changing their nature, only their extensive quantity. Nonmetric multiplicities, on the other hand, are smooth, making it impossible to carry out such operations without changing them in kind or converting a smooth-nonmetric multiplicity into a striated-metric one.

This last remark should flag up why Deleuze and Guattari's ontology, and in particular the theory of multiplicities borrowed from Bergson and Riemann, is of relevance to 'the revolutionary problem', and more broadly, a form of political analysis that proceeds via the study of multiplicities (as the quote I mentioned above on the 'change of method' refers to).[7] If there is a kind of organisation that avoids reproducing the State form, for Deleuze and Guattari it will be ontologically composed as a nonmetric or internally heterogeneous multiplicity – a smooth space or nomadic organisation that is not only 'outside [the State's] sovereignty and prior to its law', but 'of another species, another nature, another origin than the State apparatus' (Deleuze and Guattari 1987: 352).

In light of this radical alterity between the nomad and the State, it is tempting to emphasise the destructive power of the nomads and their disorganising effect – their process of 'deterritorialisation' – and valorise it in contrast to the oppressive power of a State apparatus. As Deleuze and Guattari express on many occasions in various registers, nomads propagate smooth space by breaking through the walls of striated space in order to 'add desert to desert, steppe to steppe, by a series of local operations whose orientation and direction endlessly vary' (382). Furthermore, the nomad does not just differ from the State, but 'brings a *furor* to bear against sovereignty' (352). This furor is for the purposes of undermining and abolishing the well-ordered territories of States. Nomads are thus said to be 'the Deterritorialized par excellence' (381), since their onto-ethical prerogative and political aspiration is to evade being territorialised and sedentarised, whether on a reservation or through the gradual appropriation of their smooth space by State forces.

But in drawing this sharp distinction between the nomad and the State we must be careful, for although they may differ, it is not the case that nomads are *defined by their opposition* to the State or that they live to fight it. Deterritorialisation and/or destruction of the State, Deleuze and Guattari point out, is 'neither the condition nor the object' of their existence, but at best a 'supplement' or 'synthetic relation' (Deleuze and Guattari 1987: 471). Similarly, it would be mistaken to construe absolute deterritorialisation as the defining feature of revolutions or revolutionaries, according to Deleuze. For as was illustrated above by his concern for 'the revolutionary problem', what Deleuze is after is not merely a disorganising force, but more specifically an *alternative kind of organisation* – what he hopes for is to *find some unity* of a *particular kind*. Playing up the destructive or negative aspect of the nomad can thus only take us so far – as far as the revolutionary problem: if we revolutionaries are opposed to the status quo, then what kind of organisation can and could we give rise to, and how will we be able to avoid certain forms that we find detestable? Once this problem is posed, it becomes clear that the deterritorialising effect of nomads will at most be a component within a larger strategy. Subsequently, what is needed is not a further rehearsal of oppositions – the constricting State on one side and the deterritorialising nomad on the other – but an attempt to move in-between these two absolutes in order to determine whether there is a nomadic organisation that could satisfy our revolutionary problematic.

Real Nomads

Moving beyond the opposition of absolutes towards an analysis as to the underlying nature of nomadism is made easier through a recognition that Deleuze and Guattari themselves spend much time complexifying and overcoming their dualistic ontology of nomad/State, smooth/striated, etc. While the early sections of Deleuze and Guattari's 'Nomadology' plateau focuses on clearly distinguishing the pure forms of the nomad and the State, immediately following the completion of this task Deleuze and Guattari begin to unpick and problematise this relation.[8] For example, as it turns out, the smooth and the striated, for Boulez, are not fixed spaces, but rather undergo transformations whereby one becomes the other:

> Boulez is concerned with the communication between two kinds of space, their alternations and superpositions: how 'a strongly directed smooth space tends to meld with a striated space'; how the octave can be replaced by 'non-octave-forming scales' that reproduce themselves through a principle of spiralling; how 'texture' can be crafted in such a way as to lose fixed and homogeneous values, becoming a support for slips in tempo, displacements of intervals, and *son art* transformations comparable to the transformations of *op art*. (Deleuze and Guattari 1987: 478)[9]

And it gets better. Not only do the smooth and the striated meld and alternate into one another, but they even do so while remaining the same in nature. To explain this Deleuze and Guattari borrow an example from Paul Virilio: the fleet in being (Deleuze and Guattari 1987: 387). The purpose of this example is to illustrate how one can spread oneself across the entirety of a smooth space, in this case a vector of sea, at once. Tactically speaking, a fleet of warships can have the effect of extending itself across an expanse of water, simultaneously occupying every crevice of the vector from its ability to appear at any point without prior notice. This capacity is best epitomised by the nuclear submarine, whose power to strike extends across the globe. By doing so, however, the State navy does not convert the sea – the archetypal smooth space – into a striated space. Rather, the State harnesses the power of the smooth for the purposes of State control. In other words, the smooth is employed by the State *as smooth* for the promotion of striation. The smooth characteristics of the sea are thus maintained, but they are redirected by State powers to achieve a level of control that the State on its own would be incapable of.

Here we have an excellent reason for why Deleuze and Guattari would say: 'Never believe that a smooth space will suffice to save us' (Deleuze and Guattari 1987: 500). As we can see, in some cases it clearly will not, and might even aid in the repression of nomadic tendencies, even when its nature remains unchanged. Nomadism and smooth space are thus not always easy bedfellows – a fact rarely commented on within Deleuze studies. For the point Deleuze and Guattari are trying to make here is not only that reality is constantly undergoing processes of striation and smoothing, but furthermore that it is not always so easy to tell which is which. If the sea can be striated *as smooth*, then so too can the very concrete of cities be smoothed out, to cite another example:

> [I]t is possible to live smooth even in the cities, to be an urban nomad (for example, a stroll taken by Henry Miller in Clichy or Brooklyn is a nomadic transit in smooth space; he makes the city disgorge a patchwork, differentials of speed, delays and accelerations, changes in orientation, continuous variations... The beatniks owe much to Miller, but they changed direction again, they put the space outside the cities to new use). Fitzgerald said it long ago: it is not a question of taking off for the South Seas, that is not what determines a voyage. There are not only strange voyages in the city but voyages in place: we are not thinking of drug users, whose experience is too ambiguous, but of true nomads. (Deleuze and Guattari 1987: 482)

The earlier suggestion that a space was *either* smooth-nomos *or* striated-polis was therefore somewhat misleading: it is both, as one becomes the other. In one direction, striated spaces are undone from within as urban nomads redeploy the very constructs of the city to a smoothing. And in the other direction, the power of smooth spaces is harnessed for the purposes of control. Articulating the pure and fixed dualisms of nomad/State and smooth/striated is thus only the beginning. While it might be initially convenient to abstract the two apart, this is only of use insofar as one goes on to complexify these abstractions. As Deleuze and Guattari say in the conclusion of A Thousand Plateaus:

> It is not enough, however, to replace the opposition between the One and the multiple, with a distinction between types of multiplicities. For the distinction between the two types does not preclude their immanence to each other, each 'issuing' from the other after its fashion. (Deleuze and Guattari 1987: 506)

Things are, however, even more complicated. Aside from the various tricky relations between the two types, it turns out that there are more than two types after all. If the nomad and the State are rendered 'immanent to each other', it is by virtue of a third element: the phylum. As Deleuze and Guattari understand it, the phylum is a 'phylogenetic lineage, a single machinic phylum, ideally continuous [and] in continuous variation' (Deleuze and Guattari 1987: 406), that 'simultaneously has two different modes of liaison: it is always *connected* to nomad space, whereas it *conjugates* with sedentary space' (415). For this reason, the phylum, when conceptualised spatially, is neither smooth nor striated but *holey* – the Swiss cheese of space – since it is expressed in some instances as smoothly spread and in others as contracted into a polis (413–15).

All of this is a bit abstract, but there is a political point. When Deleuze and Guattari set out their version of politics as 'micropolitics', they will do so by employing a further topological triad that will be related to this spatial setup. As Deleuze remarks in an interview on A Thousand Plateaus:

> We think lines are the basic components of things and events. So everything has its geography, its cartography, its diagram. What's interesting, even in a person, are the lines that make them up, or they make up, or take, or create. Why make lines more fundamental than planes or volumes? We don't, though. There are various spaces correlated with different lines, and vice versa... Different sorts of line involve different configurations of space and volume. (Deleuze 1995: 33)[10]

The primacy of lines is another idea that Deleuze had been working on in his days before Guattari.[11] It is, however, not until the intermediary years between *Anti-Oedipus* and *A Thousand Plateaus* that Deleuze sets out clearly his analysis of lines in an essay written with Claire Parnet, titled 'Many Politics'. Put briefly, Deleuze claims that all things and events are composed of three types of lines. The first line is the line of rigid segmentarity. These are the great segments of rich–poor, young–old, health–sickness, and so on, which dominate the easily visible and communicable aspects of our social lives (Deleuze and Parnet 2002:

126). In contrast to this line of rigid segmentation, the second line is supple. These second lines are the cracks that split through the lines of great segmentary cuts: 'rather than molar lines with segments, they are molecular fluxes with thresholds or quanta' (124). There is then a third kind of line, a line of flight or rupture. On this line, it is 'as if something carried us away, across our segments, but also across our thresholds, towards a destination which is unknown, not foreseeable, not pre-existent' (125).

So far so good – what we have here is a spatialisation of three different aspects and/or processes of existence: one that consists of our acquiescence to clearly identifiable oppositions; a second that reveals cracks in this façade and various accumulations of exceptions to the binary rule; and a third aspect and/or process of life by which we become something completely new. But now we reach a problem: how do the various spaces we have looked at correlate with these three lines? And more pertinently: *which line is the nomadic line?* Presuming that the molar line of rigid segmentarity aligns with the State and the striated, which of the latter two lines belongs to the nomad: the second line of 'mobile and fluent thresholds' (Deleuze and Parnet 2002: 127) upon which 'the most secret mutations' occur (Deleuze and Guattari 1987: 203), or the third line, the line of abstract detachment and absolute becoming? Adequately responding to this question, I believe, is of critical importance if we are to make sense of Deleuze's revolutionary politics. To do so, however, is by no means straightforward. Let me demonstrate.

In some instances the answer is obvious. For example, Deleuze and Guattari described the three lines at one point as (1) the rigid Roman State, (2) the line of the advancing Huns, with their war machine fully directed towards destroying the Roman peace (*pax romana*), and (3) the barbarians caught between the two, who pass from one to the other (Deleuze and Guattari 1987: 222–3). The order of presentation has changed here, but the nomads are clearly placed on the pure abstract line that comes 'from the east' (Deleuze 1990: 129). But on other occasions, the matter is more confused. For example, from pages 130–4 of Deleuze and Parnet's 'Many Politics' essay, the molecular line and the line of flight (crack and rupture) appear to be read together, to the extent that Deleuze and Parnet even feel the need to defend the apparent dualism that 'rigid and binary segmentarity' forms with 'molecular lines, or lines of border, of flight or slope'. And for the remainder of this essay, Deleuze and Parnet will often slip between an analysis of three to one of two (see Deleuze and Parnet 2002: 130–4, 141–2). These confusions persist throughout A *Thousand Plateaus*. In one location, for instance, Deleuze and Guattari state that 'From the viewpoint of micropolitics, a society is defined by its lines of flight, which are molecular' (Deleuze and Guattari 1987: 216). Elsewhere, however, Deleuze and Guattari clearly describe the second line as a rhizomatic line in distinction to the line of flight, where it is the rhizome that 'belongs to a smooth space' and constitutes 'anomalous and nomadic multiplicities', 'multiplicities of becoming, or transformational multiplicities' – in short, Bergson's heterogeneous or non-metric multiplicity (Deleuze and Guattari 1987: 505–6). Which line is it, then, that is truly nomadic, that belongs to a smooth space? Which of these two lines is the line of becoming, and on which line does creativity occur? The crack or the rupture, the molecular line or the line of flight, the rhizomatic line or the pure abstract line?

There is another problem of significance closely related to this question. When Deleuzians speak of the dualisms major/minor, molar/molecular, State/nomad and others like them, it is common to associate the 'major' term in each set with consolidation, stasis, identity and being, while the 'minor' term is grouped with dispersion, flow, difference and becoming (to name but a few).[12] But as we have seen above, the molar and molecular are themselves only two of three lines, the third of which – the line of flight – is also commonly equated with these same 'minor' terms. How, then, are we to reconcile the three lines with Deleuze's great dualisms? How does three fit into two, and vice versa? This problem is often glossed over and/or inadequately explained in the secondary literature. There are numerous examples, but let us briefly consider two. In his glossary of Deleuzian vocabulary, François Zourabichvili explains for us most capably the contrast between a line of flight and the process of striation, which proceeds via binary couples. He has rather less to say, however, on how lines of flight differ from and relate to molecular lines; indeed, Zourabichvili barely admits the existence of these other lines, and when he does so he is careful to omit their molecular name, preferring to call them by their other moniker – supple (Zourabichvili 2012: 179). Given that Zourabichvili will elsewhere directly relate the molecular to the nomadic and the smooth (182), this omission is certainly most convenient, as it would patently jar with the link he also wants to claim between the line of flight and smooth space (179).

In her essay 'Politics as the Orientation of Every Assemblage', Véronique Bergen goes farther than Zourabichvili in explicating Deleuze's political topology. Bergen, however, does not take note of the slippages in Deleuze's own treatment of the three lines that I revealed above; on the contrary, she reproduces them. After noting that a Deleuzian political ontology is composed of, on the one hand, the molar/molecular schema, and on the other, the three lines, Bergen proceeds to predictably align the molar/molecular schema with various other Deleuzian dualisms, such as actual/virtual, macroscopic/infinitesimal and history/becoming. But when it comes to discussing the three lines, subtle shifts occur in explication that make it difficult to understand how these two topologies relate. For example, while we are initially told that it is with molecular lines that 'becomings emerge, occurring in a non-chronological time', Bergen subsequently reveals that it is lines of flight 'that are characterised by a primacy that is ontological and not chronological' (Bergen 2009: 36–7). And as her analysis continues, lines of flight are described using the terms 'micropolitics', 'evental effluences' and 'becoming', in direct opposition to 'macropolitics', 'the state of things' and 'history' (37). It is thus not surprising that when Bergen attempts to juxtapose the two topologies, she fails to refer to all three lines. As she says:

> Mixing the types of lines – the molar being equivalent to hard segmentary lines, the molecular to quantum lines – the 'molar' and the 'molecular' compose a double mode of being, in immanence, which, in every assemblage, signals the existence of a virtual which insists as pure reserve and an actual without resemblance to the transcendental forge from which it emanates. (Bergen 2009: 36)

As we can see here, the dualistic molar/molecular schema is accounted for, but where are all three lines? If the molar term in the dualistic molar/molecular schema is equivalent to molar lines (rigid segmentary lines), then which line is equivalent to the molecular half? Bergen evades this question somewhat by referring to 'quantum lines', but which of the three lines are these? Molecular lines or lines of flight? To the best of my knowledge, the phrase 'quantum lines' never appears in Deleuze's work – he instead refers to lines 'marked by quanta' or 'with quanta'. But to be fair to Bergen, Deleuze is himself confused on this very question. Depending where you look, it can be either the second or third line that is 'marked by quanta' (compare Deleuze and Parnet 2002: 124 and Deleuze and Guattari 1987: 195 with Deleuze and Guattari 1987: 222). The same problem can be found when tracking the respective dangers of the three lines. While falling/reverting into a black hole is at times said to be the danger of the second molecular line, at others times this is the danger of lines of flight (compare Deleuze and Parnet 2002: 138 with Deleuze and Guattari 1987: 205). Thus, while it is clear that molar lines hold up one half of the dualism, we are left to wonder by Bergen and

Deleuze alike as to how the second and third lines conspire to form the other half, whether one takes the place of the other, and/or which one of them is 'becoming' if it is the molar that is 'history'.[13]

What, then, are we to make of all this confusion? Are nomads molecular, or do they instead pursue a line of flight distinct from molecular lines? In light of the shifting and/or confused presentation of the material that I have highlighted – itself exacerbated by the fact that the texts we are drawing from here were written by three people, two of whom never collaborated and could very well have penned the passages in question – we as Deleuzians are somewhat liberated to make of this political ontology-topology what we will (within limits, of course). Granted this licence, and contrary to the previous stated evidence that names the nomad as 'the Deterritorialized par excellence' and the 'man of deterritorialization' (Deleuze and Parnet 2002: 134), I would suggest that if the nomad is to be the figure of transformation, then it might in fact be more appropriate to place him or her in the continually shifting and amorphous space *in-between* the Romans and the advancing Huns. For is it not the barbarians who come closest to the ontology and ethic of transformation? The Huns are sure of their task – destruction of the State – but the barbarians, by contrast, have mastered the art of disguise and metamorphosis, continually going *between* the Romans and the Huns, becoming one, passing off as another, and then taking up arms against either or both. It is the barbarians, in other words, that are truly between known and immutable identities. As Deleuze and Guattari note at one point: 'It is odd how supple segmentarity is caught between the two other lines, ready to tip to one side or the other; such is its ambiguity' (Deleuze and Guattari 1987: 205). But is not this 'oddity' precisely the essence of metamorphosis and transmutation? Is not this 'ambiguity', as opposed to pure being or pure becoming, precisely what is so 'Interesting, Remarkable, and Important' (Deleuze and Guattari 1994: 82)? Such, in my opinion, is the virtue of this other transformative figure, or second force of nomadism, who moves between purities – the molecular barbarians, or what we might possibly think of as the *real* (but not absolute) nomads of Deleuze and Guattari's nomadology.[14]

The majority of Deleuze's pragmatic and prescriptive moments support this reading. Invariably, every call made by Deleuze for 'revolutionary becoming' is tempered with a precautionary reminder. To demonstrate, witness the conclusion to the 'Many Politics' essay (which is then replicated and developed further in the 'Micropolitics' plateau). First, dissolution of the State and the line of rigid segmentarity is not the point in itself. As Deleuze says:

Even if we had the power to blow it up, could we succeed in doing so without destroying ourselves, since it is so much a part of the conditions of life, including our organism and our very reason? The prudence with which we must manipulate that line, the precautions we must take to soften it, to suspend it, to divert it, to undermine it, testify to a long labour which is not merely aimed against the State and the powers that be, but directly at ourselves. (Deleuze and Parnet 2002: 138)

Second, to those who are too sure of their calling, Deleuze has the following to say: 'You have not taken enough precautions' (Deleuze and Parnet 2002: 138). 'Precaution', 'prudence' – not exactly the words that would support a Deleuzian politics founded on the celebration of absolute deterritorialisation. In fact, in a direct response to those readers who would overly glorify (or attack) his analysis of becoming and deterritorialisation, Deleuze remarks:

> Some have said that we see the schizophrenic as the true revolutionary. We believe, rather, that schizophrenia is the descent of a molecular process into a black hole. Marginals have always inspired fear in us, and a slight horror. They are not clandestine enough. (Deleuze and Parnet 2002: 139)

Such 'marginals', in other words, are a bit too obvious. One should not be able to identify a nomad from their haircut. If it were that easy then genuine creation would not need encouraging or protecting. This is why the question of the revolution is so problematic:

> The question of a revolution has never been utopian spontaneity versus State organization. When we challenge the model of the State apparatus or of the party organization which is modelled on the conquest of that apparatus, we do not, however, fall into the grotesque alternatives: either that of appealing to a state of nature, to a spontaneous dynamic, or that of becoming the self-styled lucid thinker of an impossible revolution, whose very impossibility is such a source of pleasure. (Deleuze and Parnet 2002: 145)

We can thus see from these passages precisely who is *not* a true revolutionary for Deleuze: both acolytes of pure flux and 'marginals' will be incapable of thinking, let alone bringing about, a 'new type of revolution' (Deleuze and Parnet 2002: 147).[15] This new type of revolution is not entirely sure of the way forward; it is not even always sure where the impediments are or who are the nomads. But it could not be otherwise, since

> we can't be sure in advance how things will go. We can define different kinds of line, but that won't tell us one's good and another bad. We

can't assume that lines of flight are necessarily creative, that smooth spaces are always better than segmented or striated ones. (Deleuze and Guattari 1987: 33)

A tempered position marked by prudence is therefore the most appealing. It is also the most difficult, and in a certain sense, the most radical: as the molecular barbarians know, there is arguably nothing harder than charting one's own path between a binary of oppositional lines. It is no doubt true that Deleuze often partakes in dualistic decisions, especially when it comes to the ontologies of becoming and being. But in the end, Deleuze always hopes to go beyond these, to itinerate between so that he can both become and defend against its dangers at the same time. This is why it is important to remember that what Deleuze calls 'the crack' (originally taken from F. Scott Fitzgerald's autobiographical essay *The Crack-Up*[16]) in fact refers to the molecular or rhizomatic line *in-between* the lines of rigid segmentary that 'proceed by oversignificant *breaks*' and the line of rupture: '*Break line, crack line, rupture line*' (Deleuze and Guattari 1987: 200). Only then can we understand the following guideline:

> Well then, are we to speak always about Bousquet's wound, about Fitzgerald's and Lowry's alcoholism, Nietzsche's and Artaud's madness while remaining on the shore? ... Or should we go a short way further to see for ourselves, be a little alcoholic, a little crazy, a little suicidal, a little of a guerrilla – just enough to extend the crack, but not enough to deepen it irremediably? (Deleuze 1990: 157–8)

Become a little bit, but not too much. Leave the shore, certainly, but do so in order that you may find a new land – do not hope to become irrevocably lost at sea. In other words, extend the crack and connect the rhizome, but do not become the rupture. When you do so, a line will be drawn that is distinguishable from both the inexpressive and the expressions of State segmentarity: a nomadic line that is *invested with* abstraction and *connects with* a matter-flow (that moves through it); a *developmental* line of becoming that is not enslaved to the incorporeal surface or corporeal depth, but is the progressive movement between them. That this line is distinct from the line of flight, yet also distinct from the striae that express and organise in an entirely different way (Deleuze and Guattari 1987: 498), once again reaffirms the middle status of the nomad that I have re-emphasised in this paper.

Conclusion

What, then, does it mean to be a real nomad or true revolutionary according to Deleuze's political ontology? As we can now see, it is questionable whether an absolute nomad placed in binary opposition to the State is capable of living up to the real nature of Deleuze's nomadism. This is because bringing down a State apparatus is insufficient on its own in responding to 'the revolutionary problem', since there is every chance (as history well shows us) that a revolutionary force will become despotic. Revolutionary forces and becomings thus cannot be simply ascribed to those who call for the Revolution and devote their waking lives to its fulfilment, for not only is it difficult to determine who is a nomad or what is a smooth space by appearance, but the nomad and the smooth are themselves susceptible to appropriation by the State and the striated. These appropriations can occur, furthermore, not simply through the transformation of what was once nomadic-smooth into something statist-striated, but even more worryingly through a maintenance of its nature redirected towards other ends. As Deleuze and Guattari warn:

> We say this as a reminder that smooth space and the form of exteriority do not have an irresistible revolutionary calling but change meaning drastically depending on the interactions they are part of and the concrete conditions of their exercise of establishment. (Deleuze and Guattari 1987: 387)

As for who are our nomads today, our true revolutionaries...? Ultimately, this is a question to which Deleuze's practice of thought brings us rather than answers – or perhaps more specifically, rephrases and reapproaches as follows: where are your lines, your breaks, cracks and ruptures? Do you recognise these lines in yourself or the various organisations you are a part of?[17] Chances are you will – if Deleuze is correct, then there is a little bit of each in all of us. And chances are that this evaluation can aid in avoiding formations that slide dangerously to one side. If we are thus unable to name names in our search for nomads and revolutionaries, what I think we can safely say is that to be a real nomad or revolutionary in the Deleuzian sense, one must be attuned to the different lines that we are composed of, maintain an appropriate respect for each of them (without collapsing one onto the other), and pursue any engagement and experimentation between them with a healthy dose of 'prudence' and 'precaution'. For it is only through such a practice that creativity and transformation can not only be embarked upon, but concretely realised in a strata of organisation that facilitates life.

Notes

1. For a comprehensive survey of the field of Deleuze and politics, see Gilbert 2009.
2. Nicholas Thoburn poses a similar question to this in his excellent piece 'What Is a Militant?' (Thoburn 2008). Thoburn's pursuit of this question takes the form of a critique of militant groups (in particular the Weatherman group) through the use of Deleuzian philosophy. My paper, in contrast, will provide a description of this philosophy, followed by a critical analysis of it, for the purposes of addressing a Deleuzian problematic. Thoburn's paper, furthermore, does not really complicate the notion of the militant, but on the contrary specifies and clarifies the figure of the militant, before going on to suggest an a-militant alternative. In distinction to this, my paper will demonstrate the complexities involved in determining the figure of the nomad, and will suggest that there might be more than one alternative. For these reasons and more,
   I would consider our papers to be both distinct and complementary. I would furthermore consider my paper to be distinct from and complementary to Véronique Bergen's 'Politics as the Orientation of Every Assemblage' (2009). As with Bergen's analysis, my paper will emphasise the significance of topology to Deleuze's political ontology. This analysis, however, will subsequently proceed to a critique of this political ontology that reveals insights absent in Bergen's paper.
3. Deleuze is, of course, not the first or last person to identify this revolutionary problem. The purpose of this paper, however, is not so much to integrate Deleuze with other literature on the topic, but rather to articulate more specifically the nature of Deleuze's response to this problematic, and by doing so complicate the dualistic tropes upon which much Deleuzian political philosophy rests, whether normative or descriptive.
4. While much of what I will describe in the first section of the paper is no doubt familiar to learned Deleuzians, I would point out that it nevertheless remains necessary to state the basic concepts and standard positions of Deleuzian thought that this paper will subsequently attempt to complexify and challenge.
5. See also Deleuze and Guattari 1987: 369, where *nomos* is opposed to *logos*: 'there is an opposition between the *logos* and the *nomos*, the law and the *nomos*'.
6. See also Deleuze 1990: 75, where nomadic distribution is explained as 'distributing in an open space instead of distributing a closed space'.
7. For further evidence of how Deleuze and Guattari's conception of the nomad/State and smooth/striated is derived from Bergson's theory of multiplicities, see Deleuze and Guattari 1987: 477, 479, 488.
8. For a fuller analysis of the Nomadology that chronicles the plateau's movements (from dualism to a triad to monism and pluralism) see Lundy 2012: ch. 3.
9. For the Boulez reference, see Boulez 1971: 87 (translation modified). For more on the dissymmetrical passages between and transmutations of the smooth and the striated, see Deleuze and Guattari 1987: 474, 480, 482, 486, 493, 500.
10. See also Deleuze and Guattari 1987: 202: 'Individual or group, we are traversed by lines, meridians, geodesics, tropics, and zones marching to different beats and differing in nature.'
11. See Deleuze 1990: 154–61.
12. For one amongst numerous examples of this, see Buchanan 2008: 16–17.

13. For one further example, see Gilbert 2009: 18. As we find here, the major/minor schema is invoked, molar lines are affiliated with the 'major', lines of flight with the 'minor', and there is no mention of molecular lines. Gilbert, it must be said, is only referring to these issues in passing, as opposed to Zourabichvili and Bergen's more direct/extensive treatments. But it is for this reason that I would bring attention to this example – for if the reconciliation of the two topological schemas is perennially passed over as a problem within the literature on Deleuze and politics, it is for the most part due to such pervasive casual references to, and uses of, the relevant terms.

14. I am willing to concede that this advocation of the molecular barbarian over the nomadic rupture is, to a certain extent, rhetorical. However, given the paucity of coverage within the secondary literature of this middle figure, in between the nomad and State, I would argue that this polemical treatment is justified. One could note, for instance, that it is far more common to find within the secondary literature on Deleuze a defence of the State and the virtues of molarity than it is to find any discussion of molecular barbarians – their positive features and their distinction from both the nomad and State.

15. Thoburn's investigation into 'what is a militant' also arrives at this point (Thoburn 2008: 114). I would point out, however, that Thoburn's route to this conclusion is quite distinct from mine.

16. See Fitzgerald 1945.

17. As Deleuze puts it: 'This is why the questions of schizoanalysis or pragmatics, micro-politics itself, never consists in interpreting, but merely in asking what are your lines, individual or group, and what are the dangers on each' (Deleuze and Parnet 2002: 143). In drawing attention to this feature, it must be noted that I do not mean to suggest that the question of 'who' is a bad one or needs replacing with the question of 'where'. While I would not disagree with commentators who suggest that the question of 'where' is of the utmost importance to a Deleuzian politics (Bergen 2009: 34–5), what my analysis has endeavoured to demonstrate is no more or less than the manner in which the questions of 'who', 'where' and 'what' are intertwined in Deleuze's thought – a feature that is perhaps most evident in Deleuze's final book with Guattari, in which all of these questions are posed and shown to inform one another. At any rate, the question of 'who are our nomads today?' is Deleuze's own question (Deleuze 2004: 260), and thus one that is presumably worth pursuing within Deleuzian thought, even if or when this pursuit involves forays into topology.

References

Bergen, V. (2009) 'Politics as the Orientation of Every Assemblage', trans. J. Gilbert, *New Formations*, 68.

Boulez, P. (1971) *Boulez on Music Today*, trans. S. Bradshaw and R. Bennett, Cambridge, MA: Harvard University Press.

Buchanan, I. (2008) 'Power, Theory and Praxis', in I. Buchanan and N. Thoburn (eds), *Deleuze and Politics*, Edinburgh: Edinburgh University Press.

Deleuze, G. (1990) *The Logic of Sense*, ed. C. V. Boundas, trans. M. Lester with C. Stivale, London: Continuum.

Deleuze, G. (1994) *Difference and Repetition*, trans. P. Patton, London: Athlone Press.

Deleuze, G. (1995) *Negotiations: 1972–1990*, trans. M. Joughin, New York: Columbia University Press.

Deleuze, G. (2004) *Desert Islands and Other Texts: 1953–1974*, ed. D. Lapoujade, trans. M. Taormina, Los Angeles and New York: Semiotext(e).

Deleuze, G. (2006) *Two Regimes of Madness: Texts and Interviews: 1975–1995*, ed. D. Lapoujade, trans. A. Hodges and M. Taormina, Los Angeles and New York: Semiotext(e).

Deleuze, G. and F. Guattari (1984) *Anti-Oedipus*, trans. R. Hurley, M. Seem and H. R. Lane, London and New York: Continuum.

Deleuze, G. and F. Guattari (1987) *A Thousand Plateaus*, trans. B. Massumi, Minneapolis: University of Minnesota.

Deleuze, G. and F. Guattari (1994) *What is Philosophy?*, trans. G. Burchell and H. Tomlinson, New York: Columbia University Press.

Deleuze, G. and C. Parnet (2002) *Dialogues*, trans. B. Habberjam and H. Tomlinson, London and New York: Continuum.

Fitzgerald, F. S. (1945) *The Crack-Up*, New York: New Directions.

Gilbert, J. (2009) 'Deleuzian Politics? A Survey and Some Suggestions', *New Formations*, 68.

Lundy, C. (2012) *History and Becoming: Deleuze's Philosophy of Creativity*, Edinburgh: Edinburgh University Press.

Thoburn, N. (2008) 'What Is a Militant?', in I. Buchanan and N. Thoburn (eds), *Deleuze and Politics*, Edinburgh: Edinburgh University Press.

Zourabichvili, F. (2012) *Deleuze: A Philosophy of the Event, together with The Vocabulary of Deleuze*, ed. G. Lambert and D. W. Smith, trans. K. Aarons, Edinburgh: Edinburgh University Press.

What Is Called Thinking?: When Deleuze Walks along Heideggerian Paths

Benoît Dillet   University of Kent

Abstract

When on the last page of *What Is Philosophy?*, Deleuze and Guattari (1995: 218) claim that philosophy needs a non-philosophy, this statement is the result of a long engagement with the problem of thinking in society. It is this engagement that we intend to reconstruct in this article. By developing an original definition of thinking after Heidegger, Deleuze is able to claim that philosophy is not the only 'thinking' discipline. Our point of departure is Deleuze's constant reference to a phrase from Heidegger's lecture course *What Is Called Thinking?*: 'We are not yet thinking' (Deleuze 1988: 116, 1989: 167, 1994: 144, 2002: 108; Deleuze and Guattari 1995: 56). This phrase points to the demand for a new distribution of the relation between philosophy and its outside. The purpose of this article is to trace Heidegger's influence on Deleuze's definition of thinking and to raise two points. First, Deleuze borrows some elements of Heidegger's definition of thinking to further his own understanding of politics as an involuntary practice. For both, the question of thinking is *political*. Second, by departing from Heidegger, Deleuze can democratise the definition of thinking, beyond its confinement to philosophy, by turning to cinema. Deleuze calls cinema the art of the masses because it brings the masses in contact with external signs. Finally, in the last part of this article, we will discuss how Deleuze raises stupidity (and not error) as a transcendental problem that should be constantly fought. In this way, we hope to shed light on how Deleuze moves from Heidegger's question 'what is called thinking?' to the problem of stupidity and shame.

Keywords: Heidegger, involuntary, thinking, politics, cinema, stupidity

Deleuze Studies 7.2 (2013): 250–274
DOI: 10.3366/dls.2013.0105
© Edinburgh University Press
www.euppublishing.com/dls

I. Asking the Question: What Is Called Thinking?

A reflection on thinking ultimately requires us to question not only the relation between thinking and being, but also to answer the question 'who thinks?' or 'who can have access to "thoughts"?'. After Heidegger, thinking has to do with ontology and this is even more true for Deleuze who decidedly follows Heidegger's uncovering of the question of being by affirming that 'philosophy merges with ontology' (Deleuze 1990: 179). Yet for Deleuze, thinking refers less to a constituted subject than to a set of singularities and processes that sometimes constitute themselves as a subject (sharing similarities with what Foucault calls subjectivation). Drawing on Simondon, Deleuze's ontology manifests itself as psycho-collective, or impersonal and pre-individual, individuations, always in the making. This Deleuzian ontology is distinct from the ontological difference put forth by Heidegger (as the Being of beings), whose project is a constant search for the un-concealing (*aletheia*) and the clearing of the Truth of Being by de(con)structing the history of Western metaphysics. Deleuze's ontology of the actual and the virtual resembles the twofold nature of Heidegger's ontological difference but ultimately differs from it. This becomes clear when looking at their political thought.[1] As we will see, Heidegger believes that philosophy founds science and that the university should remain independent from politics, whereas for Deleuze thinking happens in all disciplines, as illustrated by the example of cinema. We will attempt to make sense of Deleuze's references to Heidegger in order to understand how – from a Heideggerian perspective – he can develop an understanding of politics as an involuntary practice. The main objective of this article is to understand why, for Deleuze, politics too should start thinking. In this sense, we will be arguing that the question 'what is called thinking?' is not only crucial for Deleuze's philosophy but also for his political thought, since for Heidegger this already is a *political* question.

Deleuze left us with some indications as to how and where his philosophy meets Heidegger's. While in *What Is Philosophy?* he famously wrote with Guattari that 'it is not always easy to be Heideggerian' (Deleuze and Guattari 1995: 108), he did not hide his disagreement with Heidegger's understanding of ontological difference and the project of overcoming metaphysics (Deleuze 1995: 136). There are two places where he explicitly presents his relationship to Heidegger. The first is in the preface to *Difference and Repetition*, where he signposts that the book is, among other things, a confrontation with him (Deleuze 1994: xix). The theme of the univocity of being that lurks throughout Deleuze's philosophy draws directly from Heidegger's reading of Parmenides and Duns Scotus, while at the same time departing from Heidegger to posit that being is difference independently from identity (A = A) and the repetition of the same.[2] The second is in Deleuze and Heidegger's respective interpretations of Nietzsche. Following Malabou (2010), we can claim that shifting the interpretation of Nietzsche away from Heidegger's reading, but also, more broadly, away from any conservative and reactionary reading, is one of the main objectives of *Nietzsche and Philosophy* (2002). Deleuze discusses Heidegger's reading of Nietzsche by referring to the lecture course *What Is Called Thinking?* in a footnote (Deleuze 2002: 220), criticising his interpretation of the eternal return for remaining bound to identity and opposition. For Heidegger, the eternal return happens in life and is an affirmation against death and weakness, whereas for Deleuze the eternal return cannot be subjected to identity and the same but is the repetition of difference. In Deleuze's case, then, the eternal return belongs to a philosophy of difference that breaks with recollection as a philosophy of identity (Boundas 2009: 332). 'The Identical does not return . . . only affirmation returns – in other words, the Different, the Dissimilar' (Deleuze 1994: 299). Since repetition is disburdened from identity and representation, thinking is without an origin and a destiny; most importantly, it cannot happen 'between two things, between a point of departure and a point of arrival, not even between Being and being' (Deleuze 2004: 159).

As Malabou (2010) notes, by interpreting the eternal return as the return of difference Deleuze (with other French philosophers such as Derrida, Blanchot, Klossowski) performs 'an interpretative *coup*', reintroducing a concept that is not found in Nietzsche back into the latter's philosophy.[3] The conflict constitutes without doubt a decisive step in Deleuze's formulations that 'being is difference' and that 'to ground is to metamorphose' (Deleuze 1994: 64, 172). In brief, we find a univocity of being which is disengaged from Heidegger's thought.

Now that we have referred to the main places where Deleuze explicitly confronts and disagrees with Heidegger's philosophical project, we can investigate their common ground. Deleuze borrows the concepts of *Denken* (thinking), *Stimmung* (mood) and *Gelassenheit* (releasement) from Heidegger. We will argue that much of Heidegger's theory of thinking[4] (in relation to waiting and releasement) influenced Deleuze's conception of thinking and other practices as 'involuntary'. The emphasis placed on the involuntary is not an apology for renunciation or resentment, but rather it means that thinking and other practices must be opened up to an impersonal and collective dimension disburdened from the object and the subject. Thinking, but also other realms, such as politics, can be conceived from the perspective of the involuntary (see Zourabichvili 1998). But before we extend this claim to politics, it is important to understand that this involuntary practice of thinking is both an interpretation and a continuation of Heidegger's claim that 'we are not yet thinking'.[5] For instance, Deleuze notes in an interview soon after the publication of *Difference and Repetition* that: 'what we're looking for these days is a new image of the act of thought, its functioning, its genesis in thought itself' (Deleuze 2004: 139–40).

Although thinking can be conceived as a traditional problem since the first philosophy of Descartes in his *Metaphysical Meditations*, with Heidegger it takes on a collective, hence *political*, meaning that is taken up by Deleuze with different aims. Deleuze wants to 'renew' the image of thought *with* but also *contra* Heidegger: 'It is definitely Foucault, along with Heidegger but in a quite different way, who has most profoundly transformed the image of thought' (Deleuze 1995: 95; translation modified). The expression 'image of thought' should be read as a continuation of Marx's concept of ideology (Sauvagnargues 2010: 38), with the distorted reality here figuring as a certain 'dogmatic' representation within philosophy, a kind of false consciousness existing in philosophy. It is Marxist precisely because this dominating ideology is the result of an alienating historical development: 'An image of thought called philosophy has been formed historically and it effectively stops people from thinking' (Deleuze and Parnet 2006: 10). But equally, the notion of the 'image of thought' can be interpreted in a different and positive way, in which thinking refers to faculties other than the cognitive faculty: a sensibility and a visibility (as we shall see in sections II and V, regarding signs and the cinematic image). For Deleuze, the form of thought should be expressive and performative and not simply reduced to its content: the couple form/content of thought cannot be separated. The image should not simply be used in philosophy as an example or a metaphor, but according to Deleuze (which is arguably true for many twentieth-century French philosophers), the very expressivity found in art should also be considered. To connect thought with images, or to introduce images into thought, is to establish parallels with other spheres of contemporary life, in order to create resonances in tune with the spirit of our time. Indeed, as he puts it, 'What can be more joyful than a spirit of the time? [*Quoi de plus gai qu'un air du temps*]' (Deleuze 2004: 142; translation modified).[6]

It is our claim that the spirit of the time helps differentiate between philosophy and thought. For Deleuze, thought is simultaneously larger and more democratised than philosophy. Another example can help us make this point: in the same text 'Nietzsche and the Image of Thought', Deleuze explains that his project in *Difference and Repetition* is 'simply' to compose the philosophical treatise which synthesises the 'current thought', drawing directly from his present, which is France in the 1960s (Deleuze 2004: 142). The question of the spirit of the time [*air du temps*] can be juxtaposed to Heidegger's concept of *Stimmung*, or 'mood', precisely because it refers to an impersonal realm of affects. Françoise Dastur offers, in *Heidegger et la question du Logos* (2007), an interesting etymological analysis of the word *Stimmung* in German:

> It will be worth noting that *Stimmung* and *stimmen* come from *Stimme*, a German word from unknown origins, but whose first meaning is the voice in its juridical sense as to give a voice to a vote. *Stimmen* consequently means to make one's voice heard, to call, to name, then to be in agreement and also to be disposed, hence *Stimmung*, which has the meaning of tuning (as in tuning a musical instrument), then as a disposition, mood, tonality, atmosphere. (Dastur 2007: 113; my translation)

Deleuze seems to use the expression '*un air du temps*' in a very similar way to this Heideggerian notion of *Stimmung*, as a manner of doing philosophy in tune with its contemporary times. As Dastur quotes from Heidegger's first lectures on Nietzsche, '*Stimmung* is precisely the fundamental manner according to which we are exterior to ourselves' (Dastur 2007: 117; my translation). It is this spirit of the time that shatters the constituted subject and presents the possibility to individuate, to compose with the world as psycho-collective individuations. For both Heidegger and Deleuze, *Stimmung* and *air du temps* are ontological formations rather than psychological perceptions. For both, yet very differently, an image of thought reflects a present, challenging all forms of doing philosophy by inscribing in them a political imperative, and opening thoughts and politics to other realms as the means to a process of transindividuation.[7] In short, thinking is a dangerous and a transformative activity. In order to bring to the fore the political elements contained in this untimely question 'what is called thinking?', it is necessary to think the present against eternal and ahistorical truths. As we may recall here, Foucault claimed that this thought of actuality was first expressed in modern times by Kant, in *What Is Enlightenment?* as an attempt to answer the question: 'what is it in the present that currently has meaning for philosophical reflection?'

(Foucault 2010: 12). Before coming back to the historical determination of thinking (especially in relation to nihilism), we should first turn to the question of the role of signs in shaping the involuntary practice of thinking.

II. The Thinking Path: A Typology of Signs and Thinking as an Involuntary Practice

One of the key themes running throughout Heidegger's lectures on thinking is the process of learning. The emphasis on learning is crucial to understanding the objectives of the book, and as the translator notes in his introduction, Heidegger's 1951–2 lectures on *What Is Called Thinking?* were the first he had been allowed to deliver since his suspension in 1944 for his involvement with the Nazi regime (Glenn Gray in Heidegger 1968: xviii). Here, Heidegger claims that

> in order to be capable of thinking, we need to learn it first. What is learning?... We learn to think by giving our mind to what there is to think about... Everything thought-provoking gives us to think... [What is] [*most*] *thought-provoking is that we are still not thinking.* (Heidegger 1968: 4; original emphasis)

This last sentence is referred to again and again by Deleuze. For Heidegger, if thinking is a human faculty, it does not mean that we are currently thinking. This is the first argument Heidegger presents, that thinking is not an innate faculty but a process to be acquired over time, through a process of learning. In fact, one cannot find what thinking is or what there is to think if one does not attempt to find the 'path' to thinking (Heidegger 1969: 23).

This process of learning is also inscribed in Heidegger's reflections on the role of the university and how knowledge should be taught. This is a concern already evident in his inaugural address at Freiburg in 1929 'What Is Metaphysics?' expressed through the questions of the role and the meaning of the sciences as political questions, concerns that awaken Heidegger from his unpolitical sleep (Heidegger 2003: 24–7). The lecture series *What Is Called Thinking?* raises political concerns but from an untimely angle: the task of thinking needs to be recuperated in the age of the atomic bomb, cybernetics and technology. When Heidegger, referring to *What Is Called Thinking?*, claims that 'perhaps it is also a sign of the times that this book of all my publications has been read the least' (Heidegger 2003: 42),[8] he emphasises the importance of these lectures in his body of work, but also maintains that the political stance to be found in them is untimely and that the people are not ready to use the antidote to cure their disease.

For Deleuze, as well, thinking has to do with a learning process; it is not about following a 'correct' method but about looking for the path to thinking: 'Thought does not need a method but a *paideia*, a formation, a culture' (Deleuze 2002: 110). However, Deleuze does not fully agree with Heidegger that the concrete contemporary world is a non-thinking time and asserts instead that thinking should be democratised rather than repressed through 'correct' methods and certain institutions. This is precisely why he argues that thinking should be the work of both words and images, the image of thought.

> No one takes thought very seriously, except those who claim to be thinkers or philosophers by profession. But that does not stop it from having its own apparatuses of power... when [thought] tells people: 'Don't take me seriously, because I think for you, since I give you conformity, norms and rules, an image'; to all of which you may submit all the more as you say: 'that's not my business, it's not important, it's for philosophers and their pure theories'. (Deleuze and Parnet 2006: 10)

The last sentence of this quote admirably shows that Deleuze calls for the people to get involved in 'thought' and to refuse the division of labour between thought and action, and the competition between the two. Locating thought in the brain and in society has been a political enterprise ever since the development of phrenology in the early nineteenth century with Joseph Gall and Johann Spurzheim. What is called thinking?, '[T]he question has ceased to be a purely theoretical one. It now seems that more and more of the powers that be [*de plus en plus de pouvoirs*] also take an interest in our capacity to think' (Canguilhem 2008: 7).

Here Heidegger's argument about thinking overcomes two hundred years of mystification about where thinking comes from. To ask about the location of thought, whether 'the brain secretes thought as the liver does bile' (Canguilhem 2008: 8), is to challenge the common belief that thinking is genetic, natural and, most importantly, effortless. In fact, thinking is a natural faculty whose practice does not come naturally to us. How do we come to realise that we are not yet thinking? Heidegger explains that when we are looking for thought, we become aware of its withdrawal, which functions as 'a sign' pointing in a particular direction. 'As [man] draws toward what withdraws, man is a sign' (Heidegger 1968: 9). Heidegger repeatedly refers to Hölderlin's sentence 'we are a sign that is not read' (Heidegger 1968: 9). Surely as a rational animal, man should be able to think, Heidegger claims, yet it is perhaps because man wants it too much that he is not currently thinking.

If thinking is not a natural condition, then a necessary struggle is required to trigger thought. Again Deleuze agrees with and follows Heidegger on these points: 'we are not going to think unless... we are forced' (Deleuze 2002: 110). Thinking is not a voluntary activity but needs to be triggered by the unthought, or what Deleuze calls after Blanchot and Foucault, the outside. Collecting signs for Deleuze mostly means tracing the disjunctive relation between the sensible and the intelligible, between non-sense and sense, between unthought and thought. Only in their discord, when they are 'out of joint', can the faculties produce the new. By emphasising the role of violence and the outside, Deleuze wants to move away from the model of recognition, since the maintaining of their accord fixes the faculties. The chapter 'The Image of Thought' in *Difference and Repetition* presents the difficult argument that for 'real' thinking – that is, thinking the new – the faculties should be discordant in order for them to be raised to their transcendent order (Deleuze 1994: 143).

Deleuze also writes in *Proust and Signs* that learning how to think concerns signs, and compares the thinker to an Egyptologist trying to decipher hieroglyphs and signs, to give them sense and value. Faculties can only be discordant once they are disturbed by external signs. It is these signs that give thought sense and value (Deleuze 2000: 4). 'What is essential is outside of thought, in what forces us to think' (Deleuze 2000: 95). Thinking for Deleuze is both involuntary and always-already involves extraneous elements – what he calls following Blanchot's reading of Artaud, 'powerlessness' (*impuissance*) (Deleuze 1994: 147). This powerlessness resembles what Heidegger calls 'waiting' or 'releasement' (*Gelassenheit*), which is an involuntary disposition towards thinking.[9] By releasement, Heidegger means that 'thinking' should be learned involuntarily, that is, it does not require a 'will': 'thinking is something other than willing... releasement does not belong to the domain of the will' (Heidegger 1966: 59).

This 'releasement' also functions in the second part of the lecture course *What Is Called Thinking?* to show that language can be used not as a mere means of expression, but also as a tool to interpret and unconceal the ontological difference to be rediscovered, since 'the time may finally have come to release language from the leash of common speech' (Heidegger 1968: 192).[10] What he calls a 'releasement toward things' (Heidegger 1966: 54) should not be simply understood as the opposite of practice or of any form of activity. On the contrary, since men only 'want' to think but do not act, he calls for a releasement towards things, a kind of distancing that is already a way of acting: 'it may be that man wants to think, but can't. Perhaps he wants too much when he wants to think, and so can do too little' (Heidegger 1968: 3). In order to reach the thinking stage, one should be predisposed to it by disengaging and distancing oneself from the calculative thinking predominant in Western societies and Western thought.

III. Nihilism and Thought

It is precisely because for Heidegger thinking is a matter of remembering what metaphysical thought has forgotten, of finding 'autochthony' and 'rootedness' (Heidegger 1966: 48–9), that his project (or 'historical mission') for 'Western civilisation' is to attain the truth of Being (Heidegger 2008: 233). Thinking should be understood as part of his philosophy of history, as the project of Western civilisation 'whether or not Western thought has yet attained the ground upon which it stands' (Pöggeler 1987: 4). The 'unthought' in Heidegger is not a desire for the new, but on the contrary the remembering of a forgotten thought. By contrast, for Deleuze the unthought is the radically new, echoing another question that he will ask in a conference paper entitled 'What Is an Act of Creation?' (Deleuze 2003). This thought of the new is a necessity but a pre-individual and impersonal one. While for Deleuze thinking is about becoming outside certain (reactive) conceptions of history, for Heidegger it seems that thinking refers to his philosophy of history as a history of philosophy. This is why in *What Is Philosophy?*, Deleuze and Guattari reproach Heidegger for remaining a 'historicist' (Deleuze and Guattari 1995: 95).

'We are not yet thinking' when we look for thought only to find its withdrawal. In fact, this withdrawal of thought points to the fact that our non-thinking stage is conditioned by the nihilism that lies at the heart of modernity. Heidegger defines nihilism, through his particular reading of Nietzsche, as the loss of meaning and value in our times. As Dreyfus points out, 'the strongest argument that some meaningful practices must have survived is that without some remnant of them we would not be distressed by nihilism' (Dreyfus 2006: 352). This distress is the beginning of thinking for Heidegger, a movement towards discerning the growing immensity of the desert. This is how Heidegger links the contemporary practice of thinking to Nietzsche's diagnosis of nihilism. Heidegger notes that what Nietzsche called nihilism is an anthropological condition within history but not a specific event in the 'ontic' history, though it is an ontological condition in history as the history of Being. Nihilism is the result of the history of Western thought and the movement within Western history that has necessary links with our condition of thought. Or, with Nietzsche, Heidegger notes the devaluation of the highest values, their degeneration, their perishing and their decadence (Heidegger 2002: 166–7) and this is what the task of thinking has to face.

The overcoming of metaphysics that Heidegger diagnoses is the condition of our presence, of the history of Being, yet metaphysics does not and cannot disappear, as he insists in his essay 'Overcoming Metaphysics'. Hence his task is summarised in a lecture called 'Time and Being' as 'to cease all overcoming' (Janicaud and Mattéi 1995: 7). To stop this overcoming of metaphysics, for Heidegger, is to diagnose and reconquer thought. The condition of our nihilist times is the lack of awareness and knowledge of the history of Being; but on the other hand, memory is the gathering of our thoughts and what we should be striving for. This is what he has in mind when he claims in a public memorial address in 1955 for the composer Conradin Kreutzer:

> Man today is in flight from thinking. This flight-from-thinking is the ground of thoughtlessness. But part of this flight is that man will neither see nor admit it. Man today will even flatly deny this flight from thinking. He will assert the opposite. (Heidegger 1966: 45)

Yet, while we realise that we are 'in flight from thinking', for Heidegger, thinking is not easy and requires a certain degree of patience. This is why he then distinguishes between two kinds of thinking, calculative thinking and meditative thinking, and calls for a 'releasement toward things', defining it as 'this comportment toward technology which expresses "yes" and at the same time "no"' (Heidegger 1966: 54). But this attitude is already a rejection of the mere compliance to technology that was dominating society from the atomic bomb to the turning of logic into logistics, and philosophy into applied sciences. 'For us contemporaries the greatness of what is to be thought is too great', precisely because the current political regimes do not yet know how to accommodate with 'the technological age'; 'we still have no way to respond to the essence of technology' (Heidegger 2003: 47, 36, 37).

In contrast to Deleuze, for Heidegger, it is the task of thinking to invert this 'uprooting of man' by a returning to traditions and to understand that since the high time of Greek philosophy, there has been a decline and a regress, a desert in thought. Nietzsche has completed the history of Western metaphysics precisely because 'the wasteland grows'

(Nietzsche, qtd in Heidegger 1968: 30). This wasteland both prevents and demands thinking. The twentieth century is also for Heidegger the age of representation, the unification of the world that becomes conscious of itself. It is not a simple negation of the age of modernity that thought should accomplish but open itself to the 'incalculable', keeping the possibility of access to the truth as unconcealing. 'Reflection [or "creative questioning"] transports the man of the future into that "in-between" in which he belongs to being and yet, amidst beings, remains a stranger' (Heidegger 2002: 72). Hence, for Heidegger, thought should be a kind of opening of becoming and of newness but as the 'clearing' of Being.

Deleuze, too, speaks of the desert of thought and it is this unthought as an economy of stupidity organised by the dominating flows of capital that is to be resisted. He makes the task of thinking, both philosophical and non-philosophical, one of his prime political projects. For instance, thought in capitalism is the target of Deleuze and Guattari when they write in 1972 that capitalism organises a doubling of 'the capital and the flow of knowledge with a capital and an equivalent flow of *stupidity* [*connerie*] that also effects an absorption and a realisation, and that ensures the integration of groups and individuals into the system' (1983: 235–6). Individuals are not locked and disciplined in institutions anymore but controlled by an ever more vicious flow of money that discredits them through the creation of more debt: 'a man is no longer a man confined but a man in debt' (Deleuze 1995: 181). Using debt, a government functions to integrate and totalise the degree zero of thought, rejecting all theoretical thinking for the celebration of transparent, communicative and calculative thinking (Lyotard 1979: 15–16). Especially in the wake of the financialisation of economy and life, resulting in the economic crisis of 2008 immediately followed by what is now called the Great Recession, Deleuze and Guattari's cartography of capitalism as a flow of capital has never before been so relevant.

Following Zourabichvili (1998), we argue that the goal of politics in Deleuze is the opening of perspectives and the possible. The only way to have a politics of difference is first to start evaluating the desert of thought, to ask about new modes of life (the conditions of *real* experience). In this sense, politics needs to refer to the creation of joyful affects that increase the power to act and be acted upon. This is why the intolerable and outrage are situated at the level of politics in the same way that stupidity and shame paradoxically produce thought. What causes the possibility of an impossibility (an outside) is the intolerable opening and creation of a new distribution of the possible: 'the possible or I shall suffocate' (Deleuze and Guattari 1995: 177). This rupture occurs at the limit between thought and the unthought, where the intolerable and the shameful can be expressed since this is to accept that 'we are not yet thinking'. It is by taking into consideration the contingency of action and thought that new possibilities of life are created. While creation for Deleuze is defined as a necessity, there is not only one necessity in the same way that there is not only one truth – there is only the production of necessities and of truths. This idea of finding 'new possibilities of life' can seem abstract but it simply refers to how one finds one's necessities, one's truths and this is precisely because for Deleuze 'we only have the truths we deserve' (Deleuze 2002: 104, 110). A thought and a truth are events that are possible when they accept and enter into relations of composition with the contingencies of the given situation.

In sum, while Deleuze is clearly interested in Heidegger's question, he turns it into a new problem about truth and pedagogy. His statement that 'we have the truths that we deserve' is a response to Heidegger's question but also a transformation of Heidegger's own response, 'we are not yet thinking'. If we are not yet thinking and we are to blame for it, this blame is not a moral or dogmatic one but a reaction (it is shame) which seeks to find a way to trigger thought.

IV. Thinking in Relation to Science, Arts and Politics

In one of the most controversial parts of *What Is Called Thinking?*, Heidegger claims that 'science does not think' (Heidegger 1968: 8, 134) and argues that scientists are too preoccupied with doing what 'science does' (research) to have the capacity to reflect on its essence. This expression functions as an order-word that calls to thought. Science does not provide access to the 'incalculable', or 'meditative thinking', but remains at the level of technology as 'calculating thinking'. This also coincides with the age of representation as driving 'everything into the unity of the thus-objectified' (Heidegger 2002: 85). Only the process of thinking can unveil the essence of science since science is too preoccupied with the application and the advancement of technology. 'Perhaps there is a thinking that is more sober-minded than the incessant frenzy of rationalization and the intoxicating quality of cybernetics' (Heidegger 2008: 449). Heidegger does not simply oppose calculative thinking (sciences and applied sciences) to meditative thinking (philosophy) but he retraces the originary task of philosophy as thinking the ground and the essence of the disciplines, since only philosophy has 'access' to being. Heidegger's critique of the metaphysical–theological foundation of disciplines aims at retrieving 'the power of the beginning' (Heidegger 2003: 3; Macherey 2011: 140–89). This beginning was the irruption of Greek philosophy, and contemporary sciences have forgotten that all sciences originate in philosophy. This argument found in the controversial Rectoral Address from 1933 is extended almost twenty years later in the lectures referred to by Deleuze:

> by way of history, a man will never find out what history is; no more than a mathematician can show by mathematics... what mathematics is.
>
> The essence of their sphere – history, art, poetry, language, nature, man, God – remains inaccessible to the sciences... The essence of the spheres I have named is the concern of thinking. (Heidegger 1968: 32–3)

Thus, thinking discovers the essence of things and time, whereas the political and economic conditions of a given epoch are organised, according to Heidegger, by other disciplines (history, sociology, economics). 'To think' history is to define the essence of the domain of history and to avoid exhaustive descriptions and analyses of a given age. But, if we follow Heidegger, history cannot think itself (unto itself). Heidegger claims that philosophy grounds the sciences but that the opposite is not true (Heidegger 1968: 131), yet much of his later thought is devoted to this untangling of life and technology as the latter is seen to both enslave and open up new possibilities.

On the contrary, Deleuze responds that 'the idea that mathematicians need philosophy to reflect on mathematics is a comic idea' (Deleuze 2003: 292; my translation). This statement could be aimed at Heidegger, who does not open up all disciplines to creativity and thought. This is particularly true of his study of cinema, for which he became renowned. But he also allows dialogue between the sciences and philosophy. This was argued by de Beistegui in his *Truth and Genesis* (2004) in which, 'by turning to certain recent developments in science, from quantum mechanics to non-linear dynamics and complexity theory', and in order to remain Heideggerian, de Beistegui decided to dissociate himself from Heidegger and follow Deleuze with whom 'it is indeed possible to single out or extract a dimension of Being that is proper to physical and material systems' (de Beistegui 2004: 15).

By leaving science and all applied disciplines to the realm of calculative thinking, Heidegger is unable to imagine what sciences and technology can do beyond the technical reason and the practical determinism that certainly drive most university research activities (we could even speak of a fascination or a blindness). Deleuze finds a way out of this pessimism and *diktat* of philosophy in Heidegger's thought by democratising the question 'what is called thinking?', that is, the desert of thought (as we will later discuss with stupidity) should 'call' to each of us (Deleuze and Guattari 1995: 107).

By relating thinking to the overcoming of metaphysics, Heidegger builds a hierarchical structure of thinking. It follows that if, for both Heidegger and Deleuze, thinking is a collective and a political attitude as we defined it earlier, for Heidegger philosophy (with poetry) has a privilege over other realms. Heidegger, in the *Letter on Humanism*, presented the danger that philosophy and philosophers face when they believe that they can justify philosophy's existence before the 'sciences' by elevating it to the rank of science, but 'such an effort is the abandonment of the essence of thinking' (Heidegger 2008: 219). Therefore, he believed that philosophy could leave the realm of science and return to thinking, but why could he not argue the same for sciences and the arts (other than poetry), and organise a fruitful dialogue between philosophy and the sciences? This is precisely the significant point of contrast with Deleuze, who has been constantly concerned with opening the realm of thinking up to other spheres, or at least recognising that other realms also 'think'. We shall attempt to explain this movement through his work on cinema-thinking.

V. Deleuze's Question: What Is Called Cinema-thinking?

Cinema 2: Time-Image is a project demonstrating Deleuze's transcendental empiricism at work:

> it is as if cinema were telling us: with me, with the movement-image, you can't escape the shock which arouses the thinker in you... simultaneously posit[ing] the unity of nature and man, of the individual and the mass: cinema as art of the masses. (Deleuze 1989: 156, 162)

Deleuze's work on cinema is paradigmatic of his project to democratise thought and philosophy, believing that people cannot simply satisfy themselves with stupidity and baseness of thought, but that if everyone has the capacity to think, one should make use of it, otherwise other institutions will. 'Thought' is a category larger than the categories presented in *What Is Philosophy?* – concepts, affects and percepts, functions, that respectively philosophy, arts and science craft. Thinking is an individuating activity – in the Simondonian sense – linking the psychological and the collective, entitling the artist to believe in this world: 'the less human the world is, the more it is the artist's duty to believe and produce belief in a relation between man and the world, because the world is made by men' (Deleuze 1989: 171).

Deleuze's work on cinema develops another original element of his philosophy: the role given to the body. Doing away with mind–body dualism (Cutler and MacKenzie 2011: 58) means that the body enters thought and thought communicates with the body: 'not that the body thinks, but, obstinate and stubborn, it forces us to think, and forces to think what is concealed from thought, life' (Deleuze 1989: 189). What is called thinking for Deleuze is then transformed into a journey to the heart of the body, where the mind and the body become indiscernible, where it is no longer of any importance whether it is a movement, an image, or a word that makes us think. For Deleuze, a writer must become a seer and images must become thoughts, since an image only counts for the thoughts that it creates.

That is why Deleuze introduces a general definition of the act of thinking that he partly borrows from Heidegger, though mostly departing from him. Unlike Heidegger, Deleuze is not interested in describing the path to overcoming metaphysics, but the path to creation and the new (Smith 2007). We can now distinguish between Heidegger and Deleuze by asking the question 'who can think?'. While for both thinking is an impersonal activity, for Heidegger only philosophers can 'think', that is, can envisage the end of a metaphysical and theological foundation to philosophy, morality and politics;[11] only they can find the essence of things and disciplines.

By presenting signs – or what Deleuze calls 'noosigns' (Deleuze 1989: 279) – cinema can 'arouse the thinker in you', unfolding the involuntary (or contingent) enterprise of thinking by opening up a transcendental field that goes much beyond the history of Being to form a new image of thought. This can be created from the elements of the film-outside that shape and modify the brain. Already in 1985, with the publication of Cinema 2: Time-Image, Deleuze considered the breakthrough in neurosciences as a major event in philosophy, leading us to reconsider the synaptic connections as uncertain and non-deterministic, in short as 'plastic'. The priority given to the brain in Deleuze's work is most evident in the conclusion of What Is Philosophy? (Deleuze and Guattari 1995: 201–18), which entitles the brain to having the role of being the junction between the three planes (immanence for philosophy, composition for art and reference for science) where all concepts, affects, percepts and functions occur since it is the faculty of creation. Deleuze celebrates neurosciences so late in his oeuvre because the age of psychoanalysis was fading and the revolution in neurosciences opened a new field of inquiry and was promising to liberate the 'dogmatic image' of the brain as a centralised machine, deterministic and responding to the laws of Darwinian psychology. But it is also because the plasticity of the brain, its resilience and its transdifferentiation resemble Deleuze's own ontology of metastability and difference, that a philosopher like Malabou can take up Deleuze's work where he left off.[12] While finally Deleuze and Guattari accept that 'it is the brain that thinks and not man' (1994: 210), this falsely appears as a simple claim since 'micro-brains' or synapses are far more than the simple unification or objectification of the brain. Creation is situated in the brain but it does not mean that the brain is the 'content' of a constituted subject. Rather, it means that all synaptic connections individuate and mould being as difference.

In short, Deleuze departs from Heidegger in that despite his creative play with language, the latter is still concerned primarily with thinking in relation to the metaphysical and representational foundation, with Nietzsche in the first part of *What Is Called Thinking?* and Parmenides in the second. Heidegger's definition of thinking remains an aristocratic one: real thought only occurs in philosophy, and in 1966, he goes so far as to wonder whether German and Greek can be the only languages one can think in (Heidegger 2003: 44). On the contrary, in Deleuze the task of thinking is democratised, even in 'the art of the masses' (his definition of cinema) 'the shock wave or the nervous vibration... gives rise to thought' (Deleuze 1989: 162, 158). It occurs when the 'powerlessness' of thought is uncovered as a problem. Cinema is the art of the masses and Deleuze the philosopher of the masses, making the task of thinking available to 'the common man'. The new pedagogy is a culture not of establishing the right method to find solutions and answers, but to raise problems. As he puts it, 'we do not possess a right to the problems' (Deleuze 1994: 158), and as long as we do not have this right we will remain 'slaves':

> Culture, however, is an involuntary adventure, the movement of learning which links a sensibility, a memory and then a thought, with all the cruelties and violence necessary, as Nietzsche said, precisely in order to 'train a "nation of thinkers"' or to 'provide a training for the mind'. (Deleuze 1994: 165–6)

Just as there is not only one 'thinking' discipline, there is not only one correct way to think. Errors are not as violent and problematic as stupidity; the latter can never be fully eradicated but should nonetheless be faced and fought. For Deleuze, we need a nation of thinkers in order to democratise thought – by way of cinema, for instance – since thinking as explained earlier cannot be voluntary and contingent but must be involuntary and necessary. A new pedagogy means, for him, accounting for the multiple paths to thought since 'we never know in advance how someone will learn' (Deleuze 1994: 165).

VI. Stupidity, or Answering the Question 'What Is Called Thinking?'

It is our thesis that the question 'what is called thinking?' is doubled by a second question: 'a truly transcendental question: how is stupidity (and not error) possible?' (Deleuze 1994: 151; translation modified). Stupidity was defined in *Nietzsche and Philosophy* as '*that which it is a symptom of: a base way of thinking*' (Deleuze 2002: 105; original emphasis). Thinking then becomes a fight against the representation of truth as an ahistorical category: 'It is disturbing that truth conceived as an abstract universal, thought conceived as pure science, has never hurt anyone. In fact, the established order and current values constantly find their support in truth conceived in this way' (Deleuze 2002: 104; original emphasis). This is precisely the task that Deleuze assigns to thinking: to fight against the false problems of stupidity, philosophy must be violent and put the stupidity of our time on display, becoming by the same token *political*. Deleuze reads *Schopenhauer Educator*, by Nietzsche, as one of the best definitions of philosophy against the established order, which for Schopenhauer was Hegel, as the philosopher of the State. Even truth becomes politicised since we only have the truths that we deserve. This 'we' is truly political, a psychic and collective individuation, which is also found in Foucault's re-reading of Kant's text *What Is Enlightenment?*: 'We always have the truths we deserve as function of the sense of what we conceive, of the value of what we believe' (Deleuze 2002: 104).

Hence, if we always have the truths we deserve, we also always have the stupidity that we deserve and Deleuze gives one of his first definitions of philosophy as the discipline that should harm stupidity:

> Stupidity and baseness are always those of our own time, of our contemporaries, our stupidity and baseness. (Deleuze 2002: 107)

> [Philosophy] is useful for harming stupidity, for turning stupidity into *something shameful*. Its only use is the exposure of all forms of baseness of thought. (Deleuze 2002: 106)

Hence, stupidity should not be understood simply as the opposite of thinking; for Deleuze stupidity is a form of thinking, but a shameful one. Yet, it is crucial to understand that stupidity also helps the process of both thinking and individuating, when it is turned into a shameful condition:

> [H]ow could the concept of error account for this unity of stupidity and cruelty, of the grotesque and the terrifying, *which doubles the way of the world*? Cowardice, cruelty, baseness and stupidity are not simply corporeal capacities or traits of character or society; they are structures of thought as such. The transcendental landscape comes to life: places for the tyrant, the slave and the imbecile must be found within it...
> [A] tyrant institutionalises stupidity. (Deleuze 1994: 151; emphasis added)

To fight stupidity is therefore to fight stupidity relentlessly as a tyrannical form of thought without any hope of final emancipation. Stupidity is not the only state of thought that philosophy should fight but also cowardice, cruelty and madness. But what tyranny wants with its 'bureaucrats of pure reason' (Deleuze 2004: 259) is to 'stop people from thinking' (Deleuze and Parnet 2006: 10), to have institutions or 'thinkers by profession' who think for others. Hence the project of Deleuze is to open philosophy to the outside, to the arts and any form of vitality. While thought and life come together and should revitalise philosophy, this also means for Deleuze to repoliticise philosophy, instead of merely having the labour of pure reason and the constant search for the verification of ahistorical truths. One finds this in his cartography or topology of affects, percepts and concepts, throughout his other books, but it is already on his mind when he writes in 1962: 'The theory of thought depends on a typology of forces... We have the truths that we deserve depending on the place we are carrying our existence to, the hour we watch over and the element that we frequent' (Deleuze 2002: 110). The existence of stupidity forces us to think higher than stupidity and find things and signs that call for new possibilities of life. Not that stupidity could vanish, but the constant fight against stupidity is what gives life its fullness, allowing one to live at one's limits: 'We write only at the frontiers of our knowledge, at the border which separates our knowledge from our ignorance and transforms the one into the other' (Deleuze 1994: xx).

We always have the risk of falling prey to stupidity; just as knowledge can never be grasped but only pursued and desired, stupidity can never be expelled from our condition but gives the energy to go beyond our condition (*ek-stasis*). 'Thought understood as pure determination or abstract line must confront this indeterminate, this groundlessness' (Deleuze 1994: 275). This unthought is both stupidity as a shameful condition as well as a dispersal of singularities and affects that fascinates us.

> Thought is the highest determination, confronting stupidity as though face to face with the indeterminate which is adequate to it. Stupidity (not error) constitutes the greatest weakness of thought, but also the source of its highest power in that which forces it to think. (Deleuze 1994: 275)

It forces us to think because we are ashamed of our condition in stupidity, in this base form of thought. This fascination is not positive or negative but powerful, it gives a sovereignty and a realm of its own for thought. Some degree of stupidity is useful and indispensable for a psycho-collective individuation. Stupidity doubles thought, one cannot go without the other. Advertisements, the media and mundane conversations are needed to sell but also to create social bonds and to weave the social fabric. Without stupidity, there will be no thought and no knowledge. Feeling ashamed is also the expression that Deleuze borrows from Primo Levi to remember that the problem of fascism and Nazism remains a political problem, and that de-Nazification does not only concern Germany but 'each of us', yet not as a generalised guilt or resentment but as by being blemished, or 'sullied' (Deleuze and Guattari 1995: 107).

Deleuze also hints at the need to break away from the old model of the history of 'monuments' by also retaining non-sense and stupidity inside as historical forms: 'this is why history is no less the locus of non-sense and stupidity than it is the process of sense or meaning' (Deleuze 1994: 208). The complementarity of becoming and history functions in the same way as the couple thought–stupidity, precisely because we are never certain of the identity of each. History is not the 'error' of becoming, or becoming the 'error' of history but its unthought, becoming is located within history and vice versa.[13]

A 'thought-event' is precisely one that can be diagnosed and understood only in its conditions of possibility (its problems); stupidity is the problem of thought, it is its double that constantly threatens it. Or, in a different way, Deleuze calls for 'a right to the problems' (Deleuze 1994: 158). Aligning this argument with Deleuze's philosophy of law as jurisprudence (de Sutter 2009) is less to make stupidity 'illegal' or to draw up the right way to think than to establish 'cases' of stupidity, precedents that are already intelligible. Jurisprudence aims at creating new rights. This case-by-case approach is to recognise the role of 'user-groups' (Deleuze 1995: 170). Philosophers, artists and everyone who actualises his or her becoming-thinker shows to new generations the capacity one has to think. It is much less about the glorification of great men, than about witnessing that the outside and the *Übermensch* is present within us, through life as an immanent process.

VII. Conclusion

We do not yet know how to make good use of poststructuralist thought when it concerns not only our minority but our majority. Poststructuralist thought as practice still escapes us. We stand by Philippe Mengue when he claims that we still do not know which sense we can attribute to Deleuze's concepts (Mengue 2009: 162). This argument is especially perceptive given the situation of the Occupy Movements in London and in New York in 2011 and we cannot help but witness its complete lack of ideas and theories. Hence, what we learn is that stupidity and knowledge are never far apart from one another and always come together; that is why for Deleuze it is the mission of philosophy and the other realms that 'think' to discern one from the other.

Asking the question 'what is called thinking?' is to start talking about politics, but grand politics, where constructions of new earths and new people take place, first in the brain – not of one individual but of a 'collective'. Foucault remarks at the end of his life, trying to shift his focus from a multi-faceted theory of power to the conduct of the self and others by raising again the question of thinking:

> We need to free ourselves of the sacralization of the social as the only instance of the real and stop regarding that essential element in human life and human relations – I mean thought – as so much wind. Thought does exist, both beyond and before systems and edifices of discourse. It is something that is often hidden but always drives everyday behaviors. There is always a little thought occurring even in the most stupid institutions; there is always thought even in silent habits. Criticism consists in uncovering that thought and trying to change it: showing that things are not as obvious as people believe, making it so that what is taken for granted is no longer taken for granted. (Foucault 2000: 457)

Precisely because there are no universal criteria to define stupid institutions, stupid policies and stupid discourses, Deleuze explains that we can only be ashamed of our stupidity, but when stupidity becomes systemic, 'a veritable revolution of the dominant industrial model' (Stiegler 2010: 49)[14] is required, emerging from a new enthusiasm or 'sympathy' (Deleuze and Parnet 2006: 39). In *Difference and*

Repetition, Deleuze explains that (systemic) stupidity is used by tyrants to preserve the existing order, whereas a becoming-revolutionary shows the intolerable and demands to think political difference, or, as Foucault puts it, 'to make harder those acts which are now too easy' (Foucault 2000: 457).

Notes

1. Deleuze's twofold ontology of the real (actual and virtual) has spurred some of the most controversial and heated discussions (Badiou 2000; Hallward 2006). We can also refer to the interesting debate between Reynolds (2007, 2008) and Williams (2008) about the priority of the virtual, and the innovative response by Williams that the notion of intensity functions in Deleuze as the middle ground between the actual and the virtual. Williams's proposition is, in many ways, furthered by Nunes's (2010) political reading of the twofold ontology of the real as a 'politics of the middle', and his interesting discussion of the notion of 'dyad'. However, Nunes remains ambivalent on the question of decisionism in Deleuze and Guattari's work.
2. Deleuze devotes a long footnote in *Difference and Repetition* to Heidegger to point out that he situates himself in the tradition of the univocity of being that Heidegger identifies but he also notes their divergence on the reading of the eternal return (Deleuze 1994: 66). On the question of the univocity of being in Deleuze, see Daniel W. Smith's classic study (2001). However, Miguel de Beistegui has argued recently that Heidegger's treatment of repetition departs from Kierkegaard and a retrospective reading of the early Heidegger highlights some common points of reference with Deleuze's differential repetition; see de Beistegui 2003: 49–50.
3. Malabou points out that this *coup* was started by Heidegger and then radicalised and displaced by Deleuze and Derrida (Malabou 2010: 24).
4. We agree here with Lee Braver that in Heidegger's later writings "'thinking' is being used here as *a technical term* with a distinctive meaning rather than just entertaining thoughts or the activity studied by epistemology" (Braver 2009: 116; emphasis added).
5. A confrontation between Deleuze's concept of 'event' and Heidegger's concept of *Ereignis* (the event of ap-propriation) is much needed but exceeds here the scope of this article. It would complete our attempt to understand Heidegger's concepts of *Denken*, *Stimmung* and *Gelassenheit* in Deleuze's philosophy, since after all for both of them thinking works at the level of the event, yet in different directions. Without being able to develop further, it is important to point out that Boundas's article helps distinguish Deleuze's theory of the event and Heidegger's concept of *Ereignis* as appropriation and recollection. The sense-event in Deleuze as the creation of the new and 'the memory of the future' is to be contrasted to Heidegger's project of gathering and recollection, back to an origin or forward to a destiny. On the event see especially Boundas 2009: 328–30.
   Jonathan Dronsfield (2008) already presented a first account of the confrontation between Deleuze and Heidegger, and in spite of a perceptive reading of Deleuze, Dronsfield comes to the surprising conclusion that questions and problems are similar for both philosophers, and their work becomes then indistinguishable. While being sympathetic to the approach of not trusting

Deleuze to the letter, it seems not only unfair but imprecise to confuse the role of the 'question' in Heidegger with Deleuze's notion of the 'problem' or the 'problematic'. One could have expected references to a tradition in French philosophy (Bergson, Bachelard and others) holding the 'problem' as a central concept.

6. This is also how Deleuze defines structuralism as 'problems, methods, solutions that have a relation of analogy, participating in a free "*air du temps*", a spirit of the time, but resulting from the discoveries and the singular creations in each of the domains' (Deleuze 2004: 170; translation modified).

7. Simondon defines the transindividual as the complementarity between action (at the collective level, dealing with affectivity) and emotion (at the psychic level, dealing with perception). See Simondon 2007: 104–11.

8. A little earlier in the interview, he summarises a theme of his late writings: 'A decisive question for me today is: how can a political system accommodate itself to the technological age, and which political system would this be? I have no answer to this question. I am not convinced that it is democracy' (Heidegger 2003: 36).

9. Bret W. Davis has provided a nuanced study of the notion of *Gelassenheit* (releasement) in relation to the question of the will, by demonstrating that *Gelassenheit* is not simply a negation of the will as unwillingness, even though a sense of passivity is found within it, but could be interpreted as '"actively letting' beings be themselves" (Davis 2007: xxvii). This releasement is also a releasement from the technological 'will to will' without simply being indifference and negligence. Releasement should then be understood as a reworking of Nietzsche's will to power, and could be defined as the 'middle voice' between willing and 'not-willing' (Davis 2007: 16). I would like to thank Gavin Rae for drawing my attention to this book.

10. Heidegger's suggestion is to turn to language (Heidegger 2001: 185–208), and by way of language he wants to find new meanings for old philosophical concepts and to introduce provincial language within a more national-majoritarian language. Translation is violent for Heidegger since it is both creative and generative of thought. In his last book, Deleuze also pays homage to the extraordinary power of Heidegger's play with language (Deleuze 1998: 97–8). Even though for Heidegger, this violence is to bring language closer to its originary place and to follow the 'call' of Greek thinking, Deleuze draws a parallel between Heidegger's creative reworking of language and his own thought.

11. In the confrontation of Heidegger and Deleuze, another point to take into account is the divergence on the end-of-metaphysics thesis. A precise reading of Deleuze's explicit rejection of the end of philosophy (Deleuze 1995: 136) could be developed to contrast the becoming and the event of thought in both philosophies.

12. Malabou argues for the practical use of the recent development in neurosciences at the service of new social and political advancements. Her resistance is to the neuronal ideology that 'models and naturalises the neuronal process in order to legitimate certain social and political functioning' (Malabou 2008: 68). She continues the Deleuzian and Derridean thought of the trace, of difference and becoming by applying it to the plasticity of the brain that is both receiving and giving form. The neuronal turn that she operates is interesting and furthers in many respects some of the remarks that we exposed here. For Malabou, the outside is also included as the possibility of a 'world to come', through an 'explosion' (other than terrorists' explosions) that is necessarily creative and self-generating: 'if we didn't destroy ourselves a bit, we could not live' (2008: 74). If

Malabou can claim after LeDoux that 'you are your synapses', it is encouraging since synapses are gaps and breaks, confirming that we are Difference.

This manifests the necessity to leave the correctness of thought to accept that 'every thought is an aggression' (Deleuze 2004: 139) and necessarily a dangerous and difficult activity. Deleuze later, in 1990, explained his optimism for the liberating potential of science: 'it's for science, rather, to try and discover what might have happened in the brain for one to start thinking this way or that' (Deleuze 1995: 176), yet in 2004, when calling for a neuronal materialism, Malabou writes that 'it seems that the neuronal revolution has revolutionised nothing for us' (Malabou 2008: 68).

13. Dork Zabunyan is particularly clear on this point when he explains that stupidity is contained within thought (and its condition of possibility) whereas the error is exterior to thought, and therefore only remains an adversary exterior to philosophy (Zabunyan 2008: 856).

14. And only then 'psychopower can be thrown over to become noopolitics' (Stiegler 2010: 50), but also a neuropolitics.

References

Badiou, Alain (2000) *Deleuze: The Clamour of Being*, trans. L. Burchill, Minneapolis: University of Minnesota Press.

Boundas, Constantin V. (2009) 'Martin Heidegger', in Graham Jones and Jon Roffe (eds), *Deleuze's Philosophical Lineage*, Edinburgh: Edinburgh University Press, pp. 321–38.

Braver, Lee (2009) *Heidegger's Later Writings: A Reader's Guide*, London: Continuum.

Canguilhem, Georges (2008) 'The Brain and Thought', trans. S. Corcoran and P. Hallward, *Radical Philosophy*, 148, March–April, pp. 7–18.

Cutler, Anna and Iain MacKenzie (2011) 'Bodies of Learning', in Laura Guillaume and Joe Hughes (eds), *Deleuze and the Body*, Edinburgh: Edinburgh University Press.

Dastur, Françoise (2007) *Heidegger et la question du Logos*, Paris: Vrin.

Davis, Bret W. (2007) *Heidegger and the Will: On the Way to Gelassenheit*, Evanston: Northwestern University Press.

de Beistegui, Miguel (2003) *Thinking with Heidegger: Displacements*, Bloomington: Indiana University Press.

de Beistegui, Miguel (2004) *Truth and Genesis: Philosophy as Differential Ontology*, Bloomington: Indiana University Press.

Deleuze, Gilles (1988) *Foucault*, ed. and trans. S. Hand, Minneapolis: University of Minnesota Press.

Deleuze, Gilles (1989) *Cinema 2: Time-Image*, trans. H. Tomlinson and R. Galeta, London: Athlone Press.

Deleuze, Gilles (1990) *The Logic of Sense*, ed. C. Boundas, trans. M. Lester with M. Stivale, New York: Columbia University Press.

Deleuze, Gilles (1994) *Difference and Repetition*, trans. P. Patton, New York: Columbia University Press.

Deleuze, Gilles (1995) *Negotiations: 1972–1990*, trans. M. Joughin, New York: Columbia University Press.

Deleuze, Gilles (1998) 'An Unrecognized Precursor to Heidegger: Alfred Jarry', in *Gilles Deleuze, Essays Critical and Clinical*, trans. D. W. Smith and M. A. Greco, London: Verso, pp. 91–8.

Deleuze, Gilles (2000) *Proust and Signs*, trans. R. Howard, Minneapolis: University of Minnesota Press.

Deleuze, Gilles (2002) *Nietzsche and Philosophy*, trans. H. Tomlinson, London: Continuum.

Deleuze, Gilles (2003) 'Qu'est-ce que l'acte de création?', in *Gilles Deleuze, Deux régimes de fous. Textes et entretiens 1975–1995*, ed. D. Lapoujade, Paris: Minuit, pp. 291–303.

Deleuze, Gilles (2004), *Desert Islands and Other Texts*, ed. D. Lapoujade, trans. M. Taormina, Los Angeles: Semiotext(e).

Deleuze, Gilles and Félix Guattari (1983) *Anti-Oedipus: Capitalism and Schizophrenia*, trans. R. Hurley, M. Seem and H. R. Lane, Minneapolis: University of Minnesota Press.

Deleuze, Gilles and Félix Guattari (1995) *What Is Philosophy?*, trans. H. Tomlinson and G. Burchell, New York: Columbia University Press.

Deleuze, Gilles and Claire Parnet (2006) *Dialogues II*, trans. G. Burchell and H. Tomlinson, New Delhi: Continuum-Viva Books.

de Sutter, Laurent (2009) *Deleuze. La pratique du droit*, Paris: Michalon.

Dreyfus, Hubert L. (2006) 'Heidegger on the Connection between Nihilism, Art, Technology, and Politics', in C. E. Guignon (ed.), *The Cambridge Companion to Heidegger*, Cambridge: Cambridge University Press.

Dronsfield, Jonathan (2008) 'Between Deleuze and Heidegger There Never Is Any Difference', in David Pettigrew and François Raffoul (eds), *French Interpretations of Heidegger: An Exceptional Reception*, Albany: State University of New York Press, pp. 151–66.

Foucault, Michel (2000) 'So Is It Important to Think?', in *Michel Foucault, Power: Essential Works of Foucault 1954–1984*, vol. 3, ed. James D. Faubion, trans. R. Hurley et al., New York: The New Press, pp. 454–8.

Foucault, Michel (2010) *The Government of Self and Others: Lectures at the Collège de France 1982–1983*, ed. F. Gros, trans. G. Burchell, Basingstoke: Palgrave.

Hallward, Peter (2006) *Out of This World: Deleuze and the Philosophy of Creation*, London: Verso.

Heidegger, Martin (1966) *Discourse on Thinking*, trans. J. M. Anderson and E. Hans Freund, New York: Harper and Row.

Heidegger, Martin (1968) *What Is Called Thinking?*, trans. J. Glenn Gray, New York: Harper and Row.

Heidegger, Martin (1969) *Identity and Difference*, trans. J. Stambaugh, New York: Harper and Row.

Heidegger, Martin (2001) 'Language', in *Poetry, Language, Thought*, New York: HarperCollins.

Heidegger, Martin (2002) *Off the Beaten Tracks*, ed. and trans. J. Young and K. Haynes, Cambridge: Cambridge University Press.

Heidegger, Martin (2003) *Philosophical and Political Writings*, ed. M. Stassen, London: Continuum.

Heidegger, Martin (2008) *Basic Writings*, ed. David Farrell Krell, New York: HarperCollins.

Janicaud, Dominique and Jean-François Mattéi (1995) *Heidegger. From Metaphysics to Thought*, trans. M. Gendre, Albany: State University of New York Press.

Lyotard, Jean-François (1979) *La Condition postmoderne*, Paris: Minuit.

Macherey, Pierre (2011) *La Parole universitaire*, Paris: La Fabrique.

Malabou, Catherine (2008) *What Should We Do with Our Brain?*, trans. S. Rand, New York: Fordham University Press.

Malabou, Catherine (2010) 'The Eternal Return and the Phantom of Difference', trans. A. De Boever, *Parrhesia*, 10, pp. 21–9.

Mengue, Philippe (2009) 'From First Sparks to Local Clashes. Which Politics Today', in Constantin Boundas (ed.), *Gilles Deleuze: Intensive Reduction*, London: Continuum.

Nunes, Rodrigo (2010) 'Politics in the Middle: For a Political Interpretation of the Dualisms in Deleuze and Guattari', *Deleuze Studies*, 4:supplement, pp. 104–26.

Pöggeler, Otto (1987) *Martin Heidegger's Path of Thinking*, trans. D. Magurshak and S. Barber, Atlantic Highlands: Humanities Press International.

Reynolds, Jack (2007) 'Wounds and Scars: Deleuze on the Time and Ethics of the Event', *Deleuze Studies*, 1:2, pp. 144–66.

Reynolds, Jack (2008) 'Transcendental Priority and Deleuzian Normativity. A Reply to James Williams', *Deleuze Studies*, 2:1, pp. 101–8.

Sauvagnargues, Anne (2010) *L'Empirisme transcendental*, Paris: Presses Universitaires de France.

Simondon, Gilbert (2007) *L'Individuation psychique et collective*, Paris: Abier.

Smith, Daniel W. (2001) 'The Doctrine of Univocity. Deleuze's Ontology of Immanence', in Mary Bryden (ed.), *Deleuze and Religion*, London: Routledge, pp. 167–83.

Smith, Daniel W. (2007) 'The Conditions of the New', *Deleuze Studies*, 1:1, June, pp. 1–21.

Stiegler, Bernard (2010) *For a New Critique of Political Economy*, trans. D. Ross, Cambridge: Polity Press.

Williams, James (2008) 'Correspondence Why Deleuze Doesn't Blow the Actual on Virtual Priority. A Rejoinder to Jack Reynolds', *Deleuze Studies*, 2:1, pp. 97–100.

Zabunyan, Dork (2008) 'Pourquoi je suis si bête', *Critique*, 738, pp. 852–66.

Zourabichvili, François (1998) 'Deleuze et le possible (de l'involontarisme en politique)', in Éric Alliez (ed.), *Gilles Deleuze: Une vie philosophique*, Paris: Synthélabo, pp. 335–57.

Book Reviews

Jason Wallin (2010) *A Deleuzian Approach to Curriculum: Essays on a Pedagogical Life*, London and New York: Palgrave Macmillan.

As a field rather than a discipline, education is potentially an interdisciplinary space capable of formulating new lines of thought that traverse the boundaries of the social sciences and humanities. Work in education also potentially serves as a venue for a radical form of pragmatism in terms of its direct impact on people's lives – an aspect of the field that one might think would lead to a greater consideration of education and learning within contemporary political thought. Unfortunately, however, these potentially exciting and important aspects of the field do not often come to fruition. More often than not, the field of education is the home of rigidly conservative work that contributes towards the reproduction of an image of pedagogical life prescribed by the increasingly homogenised, instrumentalised and test-focused interests of local schools and administrators. In higher education the field is becoming increasingly weighted down by the dictates of the neo-liberal marketplace and schizo-capitalism that force schools of education to become sites for the creation of flexible labour (that is, teachers) trained under the mind-numbing mantra of 'skills and knowledge'. At the same time, the arts and humanities – once the site for some of the most innovative and important work being done in all issues related to pedagogy and schooling – is quickly being dissolved in favour of more clearly identifiable forms of 'research' that conform and contribute to the increasingly overcoded domain of formal schooling and the infatuation with profit margin. Finally, at the same time that education has seldom been the home of the invention of new lines of political thinking (unless one understands the emergence of cultural studies as a direct product of the adult education programmes in the UK during the 1960s), there is a surprising disconnection between contemporary political theory and

Deleuze Studies 7.2 (2013): 275–297
© Edinburgh University Press
www.euppublishing.com/dls

questions pertaining to pedagogy in spite of what one could argue is their mutual interdependence.[1]

As this increasingly quantitative image of education has grown in recent years in direct proportion to the privatisation of the public sphere, new pathways for thinking pedagogy and learning have become more and more difficult to come by. Simply put, there is a drastic need to reconceptualise our approach to curriculum, teaching and learning in order to confront the way that pedagogy is currently being conceived of. Jason Wallin's new book, *A Deleuzian Approach to Curriculum: Essays on a Pedagogical Life* is precisely such a project. One of the many aspects of this book that make it so compelling is the way that Wallin is able to provoke the reader to engage with and utilise Deleuzo-Guattarian inspired concepts in exploring how a pedagogical life might go in place of the commonsensical, overcoded and rigidly institutionalised representations of contemporary education. While it is true that the book is directed primarily towards disturbing the habitual imagistic conception of pedagogy and the academic field of curriculum studies (a minor field within a minor field), in true Deleuzian fashion Wallin's work on this topic has implications for a wide variety of intellectual endeavours including philosophy, film studies, music studies and, perhaps most importantly, political theory. While there have been other admirable attempts in curriculum studies to connect Deleuzian thought to education, none have so thoroughly and successfully produced the kinds of conceptual tools necessary to create new pedagogical pathways – ones that are not merely critical, but productive in the sense that they provide the kind of creative impetus that compels us to think pedagogy and curriculum differently.

The argument that is dispersed through the book in relation to curriculum studies extends out of the word *currere* – the Latin etymological link to curriculum that means to run. It is with the understanding of curriculum as a course to be run that Wallin discusses the differences between a pedagogical life that *should be run* and one that *might be run*. In other words, in light of the way that habitual forms of education prioritise the construction of a course of pedagogical life that should be followed, Wallin's book prioritises *the run* thereby opening up our thinking about pedagogy to a range of potential lines of flight that seek to escape the beaten track of developmental, functional, structural and critical educational paradigms. It is perhaps in relation to the latter that Wallin's book is most valuable. Although sympathetic to the liberatory intentions of much critical thought within education, Wallin is careful to highlight some of the problems inherent to critical pedagogy that allow it to be neatly appropriated into acceptable forms of thinking education. In other words, critical approaches to thinking pedagogy have become formulaic in their approach to critiquing contemporary trends in higher education and, as a result, insufficient to the task of remedying the problems inherent to the dominant image of pedagogical life.

In contrast to critical paradigms in education, Wallin's intention is the 'development of new concepts for pedagogy' that can 'transform the normative limits ascribed to pedagogical being' (9) – a difficult task for sure, but one that Wallin successfully takes on through an engagement with, and corresponding affirmation of, a wide variety of artistic, political and ethical forces that work to weaken the hold of the State of things in education today. Wallin's book is not a watered down approach to theorising education that one often finds in progressive educationalist approach to thinking Deleuze – the end result of which often equates Deleuzo-Guattarian thought with nothing more than the impetus to be more creative. Rather, the book is precisely the kind of active intervention and associated destabilisation of the commonsensical and predetermined course to be run that we need to confront the dominant image of education today. Wallin's engagement with Deleuzo-Guattarian thought is an active one. In other words, Wallin takes on the project of concept creation as a form of tool making in order to lead the reader through a discussion of pedagogical life via specific innovations in the areas of film, games and music.

The book begins with Wallin's prioritisation of the *one* of Spinoza's plane of immanence over the *two* of transcendent thought that marks the terrain of the Judeo-Christian God, Platonic forms, Cartesian ego and Foucault's 'ethics of knowledge'. For Wallin, the problem with transcendent thought is not so much related to the attempt to clearly differentiate right from wrong, but the way that transcendence a priori restricts ways of thought. For Wallin, particularly problematic for education has been the dominance of Marxian, Saussurian and Freudian frameworks that reduce pedagogical life to either the social ontology of the mode of production, the supposed neutrality of the structure of language or the familial Oedipal template. Again, the issue for Wallin is not so much their lack of verifiability as much as it is their power to 'capture' ontological becomings in pre-established images of the world, thus limiting the conceptualisation of difference. Throughout the book, Wallin relentlessly attacks the notion that pedagogy is the act of representing reality and thus merely posited as a form of communication aimed at showing the student the world as it really is.

In following Deleuzian thought, Wallin argues that a way out of the limitations of the otherworldliness of transcendence is through the embrace of Spinoza's *plane of immanence* that reorients a conception of pedagogical life from its already established course to be run, to one of becoming and difference. For him, 'without the presence of two ontological substances the conceptualization of a transcendent beyond would be impossible' (21). In the embrace of the two, learning is posited as that which occurs when one grasps a more accurate representation of phenomena instead of an open form of experimentation along a plane that has no ontological other.

In the world of curriculum studies, transcendent thought orients curriculum towards something to be planned and implemented. In other words, when curriculum is bound to transcendence it becomes territorialised and connected to an already identified course to be run. In the difference between transcendence and the plane of immanence, the concept of *currere* is construed as either a predetermined planned course of action or as an open field of deterritorialised potential. For Wallin, the claim of what *ought* to be run is bound to the work of negation where

the reactive image of currere is figured, as much like the image of the race-track, within its own circumlocutionary negative feedback loop. In practice this negative feedback system confirms its identity $(x = x = \text{not } y)$ by establishing specific parameters of control that discontinue virtual deterritorializations or rogue lines of flight. (33)

Transcendence and the labour of the negative in the form of unhappiness, representation and reduction are replaced by Wallin with the affirmative qualities of joy, liberation and creation. If education is here understood as the reorientation of habit, the state of things is not to be replaced with an alternative representational image of the world as it should exist, but rather with the way it might exist through the embrace of exploration, experimentation and chance. In regard to the affirmative, Wallin argues that what is important in thinking experimentation in the context of curriculum is that we not limit our thinking to the mere 'renunciation of stability', but rather that which renounces all a priori/foundational thinking, whether that emerges from a commitment to the future as a goal to be reached or as a never ending becoming. In both cases, Wallin argues that what is predetermined always imagines curriculum through the lens of the death drive – being as a 'fixed' location fuelled by the desire for identity. Whether that identity takes the form of a true representation or a permanent flow is irrelevant.

The avoidance of such territorialisation is a difficult undertaking, and one that for Wallin necessitates a commitment towards the affirmation connected to the 'powers of the false' – the term Deleuze (2006) utilised in reference to Nietzsche's 'eternal return of the same'. For Deleuze, Nietzsche's teachings of joy, difference and chance are what needs to be affirmed, not the repetition of a pre-constituted image of reality. 'The powers of the false thus become a "practice" of the affirmation of difference that inheres to repetition' not the identitarian logic of the death drive typified in the educational obsession of repeating (40). The 'eternal return of the same' should not be understood as everything always returning as it was before, but rather that difference is always returning and needs to be affirmed in each instance.

As a result, Wallin utilises the Deleuzian simulacrum as a potential way to outmanoeuvre the rigidity of the most readily available image of pedagogical life. For Wallin, '[I]n the Deleuzian positive simulacrum of virtual immanence and difference, the powers of the false mark the creation of counteractualities' (38). Following Massumi (1987), Wallin continues by adding that 'the false might be constituted as a working simulation injected into a society. Here the law is a transcendent truth that underlies reality while the powers of the false work to undermine that reality by seducing the conceptualization of another' (38).

Key here is the commitment to minoritarian production – that kind of unofficial production lying outside of the habitually acknowledged and accepted forms of pedagogy and that sometimes serves as a deceptive simulation of another life. Minoritarian forms of production are what actively bring foreignness to the familiar through an introduction of 'heterogeneity and variation' into the everyday (39). In the case of curriculum studies, minoritarian thought is that which opens up our thinking about pedagogy to a range of artistic mediums not commonly accepted as appropriate ways of engaging with and imagining education. Wallin's intervention into our thinking about pedagogy occurs in two primary ways: first, it aims to bring attention to the kinds of creative interventions often discounted a priori from the scope of pedagogical life; and second, it aims to focus our attention on those specific examples that, like the power of the false, seduce us into a defamiliarisation with what has become most commonplace. As a result, Wallin makes use of specific examples in film, games and music in producing what he calls a 'holey curriculum' – an example of *currere* that relies on minoritarian nomadic, rhizomatic and schizo creations in the process of considering a different form of pedagogical life that might be run. Instead of the unhappiness of 'moribund' repetition, Wallin leads us towards 'play and artifice'.

Following Rajchman's (2000) conviction that the task of liberation today cannot be limited to a mere position of criticality, Wallin puts forth a number of minoritarian creations that potentially serve as affirmative and revolutionary forms of invention (121). Wallin engages with Jim Jarmusch's films *Dead Man* (1995) and *Ghost Dog* (1999); Todd Haynes's film about Bob Dylan titled *I'm Not There* (2007); the Japanese game Go, the artistic movement *parkour* and various hacking video games; and the most conceptually inspiring forms of improvisational jazz. For Wallin, all of these minoritarian creations serve as examples of an affirmative pedagogy. Respectively, they act as an 'ethics of singularity' and anti-institutional *enculage* or buggery; a body without organs; forms of anti-State deterritorialisation and creative becoming; and an improvisational circuit breaker that works to create a vital life.

With every example Wallin goes into vivid detail, describing the ways that he imagines each of these forms of minoritarian production working against what he refers to as the 'tyranny of overdetermination' – those rigid, predetermined and striated lines of thought that leave the state of things completely intact. In contrast to such pedagogical orientation, the minoritarian creations that Wallin utilises and holds up as affirmative anti-images and examples of how pedagogical life *might go* find common ground in the way that they 'move in difference from the determinations of habit, memory, routine, and the practices of identification in which the individual is often caught' (117).

Although most of Wallin's book is directed towards making connections between artistic creations and new forms of pedagogical thought, he does present us with a couple of specific examples of 'schooling' that resonate with Deleuze's intent to undermine the violence of representational thought. One example comes in the form of the *currere* in A. S. Neill's (1993) Summerhill School that serves as an example of how a pedagogical life *might go*. At Summerhill School there are no bosses; students are free to choose the classes and lessons they attend; delinquency does not necessitate a disciplinary response; and students are fully engaged in decision-making processes free of any formal disciplinary or moral code (180). Most importantly for Wallin, these various aspects of Summerhill exemplify a pedagogical life not driven by the assumption of lack on the part of its students, but instead are constitutive of 'a counter fascist site of desire-engineering capable of collapsing the hierarchical organ-ization of the mechanical school... releasing the machinic potentials of a pedagogical life from its identitarian or representational mechanics' (180). One might well consider this example of pedagogical life as a form of anti-schooling that puts Summerhill, as well as Wallin, within an anarchist tradition in educational thought that runs through the work of William Godwin (1793), Ivan Illich (1971) and, more recently, Jacques Rancière (1991) among others.

It is Summerhill's approach to pedagogical life that, for Wallin, 'queers' the predominant image of State-run schooling. Here the author imagines a 'queer machine' for curriculum theorising that emerges out of a 'machinic ontology' that moves towards relations and replaces the component-oriented mechanical image of pedagogical life (179). In the case of Summerhill, pedagogy is oriented towards the freeing up of the 'desire-engineering' of its students and not the carrying out of a predetermined map of how learning ought to go. The 'queering' of curriculum is thus based on releasing the potential of new relationships and connections that act to spur the creation of subjectivities prohibited within the domain of the dominant image of schooling.

In much the same way that Summerhill works to create new conceptual relationships regarding how a pedagogical life might go, Wallin's book compels curriculum theorists to create new concepts that can change the trajectory of our thinking about pedagogy. He asks how we might

> think the concept as a *metallurgical* probe-head for creating, registering, and linking viroid lines of flight. In this way, the technics of the concept become intimate to the composition of a *queer machine* for stealing *a* life back from *life in general*. (187; original emphasis)

Wallin's utilisation of the concept of *currere* as a course that *may be run* is an effective example of such an intervention that is bound to the relationality inherent to machinic thought. It is 'the ethical undoing of norms' that machinic thinking provides that allows pedagogical thought to escape the *ought* for what *may be*.

In the midst of the exceptional way that Wallin is able to utilise the thought of Deleuze in thinking through some of the most pressing issues facing contemporary schooling and the state of education today, there are a few questions that emerged while reading the book. The first has to do with the relationship between creativity, learning and disciplinarity. Specifically, what is the role of discipline in the creation of a pedagogical life not bound to pre-constituted images? Might we also be able to think of strict disciplinarity as an impetus to creation? Although Wallin states on multiple occasions that to engage with Deleuzian thought is not to advocate a permanent form of deterritorialisation, there are times when the critical role that territorialisation might play seems to be ignored. For example, in the case of music and discussion of the potential pedagogical import of improvisational music, the discipline and even preparatory training required to produce those rare cases of improvisation that Wallin seeks to utilise in the service of a pedagogical life seem to go unmentioned. If, against the goal of sonic unity in music and life, we need to 'allow the strands to sing polyphonically and pray that, on occasion, they glow white hot from within' (Aoki, qtd in Wallin 2010: 65), one wonders what role exists for disciplinarity and territorialisation in terms of preparing for the potential of a genuine form of improvisation to emerge. Second, in what ways would a Deleuzian inspired curriculum and pedagogical life work at various age levels in schools or elsewhere? In other words, how might we engage with Deleuze as teachers, researchers, curriculum theorists or concerned community members who are thinking about education and curriculum in terms of toddlers as well as high school students? How might we be able to utilise Wallin's discussion of pedagogical life of a course that *may be run* across various age groups where individual engagement with the world is not always the same? Finally, what is the relationship between a Deleuzian inspired curriculum and institutional settings? More specifically, is what Wallin calls a 'libratory' form of pedagogy possible within the school? Or, as might be imagined, is such education only possible within the context of what Ivan Illich (1971) called a 'deschooled society'?

   In conclusion, Wallin's book makes a major contribution to the field of curriculum studies and leaves readers much to consider in terms of our approach to pedagogy, curriculum studies and its relationship to political thought. At a time when most thinking about education plods along with its continued dependence on critical, linguistic, structuralist and developmental approaches to learning and pedagogy, Wallin's intervention into the field could not be more *untimely* in the way that the book acts as a disturbance against our habitual orientation of what constitutes a pedagogical life. If work in the field of education is to inspire new approaches to pedagogy and learning and thus bring to fruition some of the above mentioned potentialities of the field, then curriculum studies needs the kind of engagement with artistic innovations and concept creation exemplified in this book.

Matthew Carlin
Pratt Institute
DOI: 10.3366/dls.2013.0106

Note

1. Besides Jacques Rancière's *The Ignorant Schoolmaster* (1991) and Alain Badiou's short essay on education in *Handbook of Inaesthetics* (2005) there has been a scarcity of new forms of creative intervention into the crossover between politics and education. The hesitation on the part of political theorists to engage with the question of education is, I believe, worthy of some consideration and thought. As Wallin points out in this book, one semi-recent exception to this rule is Félix Guattari, who did show some interest in A. S. Neill's (1993) *Summerhill School* and Fernand Oury's Group for Therapeutic Education. Deleuze, on the other hand, rarely discussed education directly. One of Deleuze's (1989) few references to education seems to exists in what he called the 'pedagogy of the image' – a concept that he borrowed form Serge Daney's work for the French film journal *Cahiers du Cinema*.

References

Badiou, Alain (2005) *Handbook of Inaesthetics*, Stanford: Stanford University Press.
Dead Man, motion picture, written and directed by Jim Jarmusch. USA: Miramax Home Entertainment, 1995.
Deleuze, Gilles (2006) *Nietzsche and Philosophy*, New York: Continuum.
Ghost Dog: The Way of the Samurai, motion picture, written, directed and produced by Jim Jarmusch. USA: Artisan Home Entertainment, 1999.
Godwin, William (1793) *Enquiry Concerning Political Justice*, Oxford and New York: Woodstock Books.
Illich, Ivan (1971) *Deschooling Society*, New York: Harper and Row.
I'm Not There, motion picture, written and directed by Todd Haynes. Canada: Alliance Films, 2007.
Massumi, Brian (1987) 'The Simulacrum According to Deleuze and Guattari', available at < http://www.anu.edu/HRC/first_and_last/works/realer.htm > (accessed 17 June 2007).
Neill, A. S. (1993) *Summerhill School: A New View of Childhood*, New York: St. Martin's Press.
Rajchman, J. (2000) *The Deleuze Connections*, Cambridge, MA: MIT Press.
Rancière, Jacques (1991) *The Ignorant Schoolmaster*, Stanford: Stanford University Press.

Steven Shaviro (2009) *Without Criteria: Kant, Whitehead, Deleuze, and Aesthetics*, Cambridge, MA: The MIT Press.

Imagine postmodernism without simulacra, virtuality or deconstruction, but instead with affirmation, passion and a continual emergence of the new. But wait – fantasy, myth and fabulation belong to fiction and art – not to philosophy, at least, not traditionally. And yet, as you may know, philosophy after Deleuze has meant exactly the opposite. Open to experimentation and speculation, today's philosophers are not compelled to speak within classical divisions between art and science, or technology and the humanities. In fact, philosophers are encouraged to think of themselves as artists, 'creating concepts', as Deleuze and Guattari put it, and vice versa. Moreover, as philosophy fuses with disparate cultural practices and intellectual specialisations (all but enforced in a culture drunk on interdisciplinarity), philosophers can simultaneously think about the history of the field, its predecessors and its future, and do so with passion, emotion and creative visions of what is to come. This is precisely what we find in Wayne State University's DeRoy Professor of English, Steven Shaviro's recent book, *Without Criteria: Kant, Whitehead, Deleuze, and Aesthetics*, published in 2009 with the MIT Press.

The stakes of the project: to rethink postmodern theory – and in particular aesthetics – from the point of view of Whitehead instead of Heidegger. Philosophy from Plato to Heidegger has tended towards '*anamnesis* (reminiscence) and *alatheia* (unforgetting), towards origins and foundations, [and] towards the past rather than future' (71). Whitehead refreshingly breaks with this, showing something new. For this reason alone the text is worth a read, though the intricacies of his break and their importance for constructivist philosophies of the future make Shaviro's clear, eloquently written and insightful book that much more compelling.

Cut to the task at hand, Shaviro's analysis focuses on those aspects of Whitehead's work dealing with aesthetics, beauty, affect, innovation, creativity, his Enlightenment roots and especially his engagement with Kant (143). His critical method involves rereading Kant though Whitehead, and Whitehead through Deleuze. At first, Whitehead appears more like Deleuze than himself, and this is confusing, but such blurring of authorial boundaries is a part and parcel of the technique that many readers will (most likely) recognise as one borrowed from Deleuze. In his time, Deleuze often brought different philosophers into conversation, a process he provocatively termed 'buggery', to describe the way he sneaked in behind an author to reread and rewrite his or her ideas, producing an unrecognisable and monstrous offspring (6). In reference to his own work, Shaviro coins his three-way (between Kant, Whitehead and Deleuze) a 'relay'. Considering the goal – to create a constructivist philosophy for postmodernism (versus simply locating broken origins) – the choice of critical methods is more than par for the course.

In this review I will first discuss Shaviro's analysis of Whitehead and Heidegger, introducing some subtleties of Shaviro's arguments (via Whitehead, Deleuze and Kant) on metaphysics and aesthetics, and then pause and question whether an aesthetically grounded constructivist philosophy is, in fact, *without criteria.*

Shaviro opens in the spirit of Deleuze proper, posing a 'Philosophical Fantasy' for the future of the field. But reality comes first: on one hand Heidegger asks, 'Why is there something rather nothing?' and on the other hand, Whitehead asks, 'How is it that there is always something new?' What it would it mean if the latter question, not the former, had laid the foundation for postmodern thought? Even in consideration of only these two very basic questions, evidence of the distinction between the two thinkers becomes clear. For Heidegger, *that* anything appears at all is always measured against its absence. But for Whitehead, the phenomenon of newness is creative. Newness is continual, affirmative and essential. Further exploration of the differences between the two reveals not only the complexity of Shaviro's project, but also the tweaking and twisting of thought required for such imaginings.

Both books *Being and Time* (1927) and *Process and Reality* (1929) speak to a crisis in modernity, and address the immensity of scientific and technological change, the dissolution of old certainties and the horrors of war. Both texts are anti-essentialist, anti-positivist, and are actively engaged in working out new ways to think, do philosophy and exercise our 'faculty of wonder' (i). However, the similarities are outweighed by the dramatic differences between the two thinkers.

Consider again the distinction between the tendency to return to origin and error versus the embrace of the creative and the new. This difference is reiterated in their respective approaches to history. Where Heidegger's work is concerned with locating the 'point where it went wrong', where 'possibilities were closed down', Whitehead, on the contrary, 'mines history for unexpected twists' (ix). Heidegger's thesis that the human subject is not only constituted by, but is also eternally haunted by, the enigmas of language, is well known. As he puts it in 1947, 'Language is the house of Being. In its home man dwells...' (Heidegger 1993: 222). In contrast, Whitehead 'warns against' exaggerating the importance of language and consistently points to its 'incapacities' (x). Language enslaves; in its matrix of expression there is only one way out: through paradox that requires one to remember lost and long-forgotten origins. Embrace of the new neutralises this prison house of being and instead pushes forward towards the future.

Shaviro poses a hard and fast distinction on the subject of science and technology. In short: Heidegger is against it, Whitehead for it. Perhaps this is generally accurate; nonetheless I want to introduce a friendly amendment. While Heidegger warns of the dangers of technology and enframing (*Gestell*), his judgements of modern technology as such may not be intrinsically negative. What I am suggesting is that Heidegger's supreme danger is the inability to *question towards truth*, in which case the danger and responsibility falls on the *human*, not on technological determinism. Regardless, it is undeniable that Heidegger 'demonizes science' (x). There are many examples throughout Heidegger's work, though to accept Shaviro's point here, one need only consider this statement: 'Color shines and only wants to shine. When we analyze it in rational terms by measuring its wavelengths, it is gone' (Heidegger 1993: 172).

Such demonisations are absent in Whitehead, who holds that, the 'red glow of the sunset should be as much as a part of nature as are the molecules and electrical waves by which men of science would explain the phenomenon' (Whitehead, qtd in Shaviro 2009: 144–5). Where phenomenologists focus exclusively on the former (Heidegger, Husserl) and scientists on the latter, Whitehead's metaphysics insists on a consideration of both (145). For Whitehead, science and technology are neutralised and treated as 'abstractions' that are not in themselves negative but merely simplifications and reductions that are necessary parts of life. The danger arises when these reductions are extended into situations 'beyond their limits, pushing them into realms where they no longer apply' (x).

In terms of representation – the holy grail of critical theory – Heidegger notoriously sets the stakes of the impossibility for anything to 'stand forth in [its] being' (xi), a thesis from which postmodernism, post-structuralism and cultural studies have made their bread and butter. Interestingly, Whitehead agrees with Heidegger to the extent that, from Descartes on, Western philosophy has privileged 'clear and distinct' conscious perception (what Whitehead calls 'representational immediacy') at the cost of affect, embodiment and a consideration of the ways 'perception is already grounded in the body' (xi). The distinction being, for Whitehead, that this everyday lack of clarity is the accepted and welcome ground from which his metaphysics is borne.

While metaphysics cannot be boiled down to any single project or person, there are schools. Heidegger's general project has been to seek a way out of the classical, Western metaphysics that began with Plato and Aristotle. Whitehead, however, does not cast away metaphysics at all. Instead, he simply does it. Subjectivity is central to understanding Whitehead's metaphysics because the subject, in his view, is always already embedded in the world. This may seem akin to Heidegger's concept of 'thrownness' – denoting the factical state of having fallen in the world – but remember, in falling, a subject is drawn back into concealment, into another place and awareness that is *not* of the world. In contrast, for Whitehead, the subject is an 'irreducible part of the universe, of the way things happen. There is nothing outside of experience.' There is no before or after (as in *Being and Time*), only spontaneous configurations and exchanges between data and subjects. As Whitehead puts it, the subject, 'constitutes itself in and through experience; and thereupon it perishes, entering into the 'objective immortality' of a being a 'datum' (Whitehead, qtd in Shaviro 2009: xii).

Whitehead held that the great accomplishment of Kant was not that he placed the subject at the centre of experience (aka Kant's 'Copernican turn'), but rather, that he was the first to conceive of *experience as a constructive process* (47). Kant knew it was impossible to know 'things in themselves', so the alternative he came up with was to glean knowledge of the *how*: the *ways* one is 'involved with whatever it is that we experience or observe'. In this move, the doors opened for post-Kantian philosophy to shift the focus from the epistemological 'what' to the ontological 'how', which also meant philosophy opened itself to singularity and the new. Even though Kant did not go through this door, he nonetheless constructed (fabricated?) the frame.

Whitehead's metaphysics begins in this new space of process and change. Instead of explaining subjective experience through Kant's 'transcendental unity of apperception', Whitehead inverts the supposition and argues that experience moves from objectivity to subjectivity. Emotions do not cause bodily states, he argues; the bodily states come first and the emotions arise out of them (58). Shaviro contextualises this thesis within the tradition of American pragmatist, William James, who also rejects the conventional dualism between mind and object (20). For both, there is no 'stable and essential distinction' between the two. Whitehead proposes further indistinctions between the living and the dead, the human and nonhuman (what postmodernists call 'blurring the boundaries').

The thesis seems retroactively in line with (some) of the ideas emerging in speculative realism and object oriented philosophy today.[1] Indistinctions and anti-essentialist claims about distinctions between life and death pull the carpet out from the anthropocentrism rampant in Western philosophy (primarily in the work of Descartes, Kant, Hegel, Husserl and Heidegger). This has also been the project of Deleuze and Guattari, Foucault and, more recently, Quentin Meillassoux and Graham Harmon. Harmon and Whitehead, in particular, appear to lock in step with their treatment of the non-human subject. For Whitehead, the subject may be a 'a dog, tree, mushroom, or a grain of sand' (xii) and similarly, in Harmon's object-oriented reinterpretation of Heidegger's work, 'crystal-effects' may be included in his reconception of Heidegger's otherwise anthropocentric and romantic Dasein (human subject). For Harmon, all subjects, whether human or rock, are a part of the 'equipmental contexture' (Harmon 2002: 30), decentring the privileged role of the human in Heidegger's philosophy. There are many, obvious differences between Whitehead and Harmon (and object-oriented philosophy and Whitehead's metaphysics), which must be expanded upon elsewhere.

A constructivist philosophy, or 'critical aestheticism', emerges in Shaviro's rereading of Kant's Analytic of the Beautiful. Instead of looking to the Sublime as *the* definitive moment of rupture, after which one endlessly speaks of impossibility and interpretation (the thesis of choice for postmodernism, poststructuralism and deconstruction alike), in the Analytic of the Sublime a new ground of singular, subjective and aesthetic experience is offered. On this point, the three – Deleuze, Whitehead and Kant – meet. All concur that aesthetic experience is non-personal and singular. In fact, aesthetic experience is so singular and new, it has no foundation at all, and 'offers no guarantees' (1). Herein lies the new ground for a constructivist philosophy, *without criteria*.

Perhaps as a response to the rise in cognitive science or simply the stakes of aesthetics after Rousseau and Goethe, in vogue today is philosophy that prioritises affect as central, if not as precedent, to cognition. On this point, Shaviro finds a surplus of allies. First and most obvious are Deleuze and Guattari. Second is Rancière (only briefly referenced in the book), whose 'poetic regime' abolishes hierarchies and pragmatic criterion, allowing for the proliferation of art and aesthetics in a society based on the 'primacy of fiction' (Rancière 2004: 83). There is also Fredric Jameson who, a decade earlier, argued that all cultural production had become a form of aesthetic production (Jameson 1991). One may also include Debord and Baudrillard, whose theories of the society of the spectacle and the primacy of the visual image equally support the primacy of affect in cultural and aesthetic experience.

But can we (and I mean readers) consider feelings as equivalent to affect? For Shaviro, the answer is a big yes. 'To feel something is to be affected by that something' (58). 'Only after the subject has constructed or synthesized itself out of its feelings... can [it] go on to understand the world – or change it' (15). Feeling may be defined in such ways in dictionaries, but it is not the way it is used by Deleuze and Guattari. For them, affect is not analogous to feeling. While both feeling and affect are emotions, there is an important distinction. Feelings, or 'sentiments', are considered personal, or territorialised forces, 'feelings become uprooted from the interiority of a subject' (Deleuze and Guattari 1972: 356), whereas affects are more free-floating, pre-personal, intensities. They expand:

> Affects... relate only to the moving body itself, to speed and compositions of speed among elements. Affect is the active discharge of emotion, the counterattack, whereas feeling is always displaced, retarded resisting emotion. Affects are projectiles just like weapons; feelings are introceptive like tools. (Deleuze and Guattari 1992: 441)

To be fair, Shaviro's conflation of affect and feeling is justified by his reading of affect through Whitehead, for whom feeling is not actually feeling (in Deleuze and Guattari's sense). For Whitehead, an 'act of feeling is an encounter–a contingent event, an opening to the outside–rather than an intrinsic, predetermined relationship' (62). That is, feeling is conceptually on par with affect–both remain open, new, and impersonal. Whitehead-feelings–like affect–are abstract and unformed, 'vector transmission[s]', constituting the a priori conditions for understanding and cognition. Affect and feeling pave the road for diverse, novel entities: the 'ultimate metaphysical ground for everything' (Whitehead, qtd in Shaviro 2009: 62, 149).

And just how far does this fantasy go? For Shaviro, there are no limits. The 'new biology, as much as any new work of art', he writes, 'requires us to abandon everything we think we know, and make singular judgments that cannot be subsumed under preexisting criteria' (16). Readers must decide for themselves if it is even possible to do something like this (one wonders about history, the persistence of memory and the psyche), and furthermore, whether this new groundless-ground of aesthetics, once cleared by Kant, is not already filled with new interiors–a new carpet perhaps–woven with free-floating affect, sensation and physiology. Is without criteria really without criteria, or just certain kinds of (cognitive, rational and categorical) criteria? Either way, this minor and tangential afterthought should by no means deter from the highly significant and important project Shaviro has brought to the table.

Before concluding, a quick note on God. Like feeling and metaphysics, for Whitehead, God is not God in the conventional sense of the term. For him, God is the 'secularization of God's function in the world' (Whitehead, qtd in Shaviro 2009: 105). God is a 'God without a religion', one which is a 'force for novelty, precisely because he does not determine the actual course of events' (135). This is not so much

Leibniz's God of 'best possible worlds', nor Spinoza's privileged God (99–102), so much as it is a God that is (structurally) analogous to Deleuze and Guattari's Body without Organs: a 'recording surface, a site of inscription... "an enormous undifferentiated object... the unproductive, the sterile, the unengendered, the unconsumable"' (124). Whitehead's God – like the Body without Organs – cannot be used as an excuse or 'fallback explanation' for the conditions created by human beings: 'God accounts for nothing and excuses nothing' (139).

God, then, like aesthetic experience and the Body without Organs, is like a modulator interfacing between data and (non-necessarily) human subject – always open to the new and change. People make science, technology, art and war, not God, language or technology. In the information age, a philosophical fantasy that makes philosophy look more science fiction by way of realistic, down-to-earth insight is, to be sure, a philosophy worth paying attention to.

Carolyn L. Kane
New York University
DOI: 10.3366/dls.2013.0107

Note

1. While Shaviro does not make this link in *Without Criteria*, he has done so as an afterthought in his blog.

References

Deleuze, Gilles and Félix Guattari (1972) *A Thousand Plateaus*, trans Brian Massumi, Minneapolis: University of Minnesota Press.

Deleuze, Gilles and Félix Guattari (1992) *A Thousand Plateaus*, trans. Brian Massumi, New York: Continuum.

Harmon, Graham (2002) *Tool-Being: Heidegger and the Metaphysics of Objects*, Peru, IL: Carus Publishing.

Heidegger, Martin (1993) *Basic Writings from Being and Time (1927) to The Task of Thinking*, ed. David Farrell Krell, San Francisco: HarperCollins.

Jameson, Fredric (1991) *Postmodernism, or The Cultural Logic of Late Capitalism*, Durham, NC: Duke University Press.

Rancière, Jacques (2004) *The Politics of Aesthetics: The Distribution of the Sensible*, trans. Gabriel Rockhill, London: Continuum.

Ian Buchanan and Patricia MacCormack (eds) (2008) *Deleuze and the Schizoanalysis of Cinema*, London: Bloomsbury Publishing.

As with Foucault's famous quote, printed on the cover of *Negotiations*, if one should choose to call oneself 'Deleuzian' it is always with a sense of irony and paradox. To apply Deleuze is not to be 'Deleuzian' in the sense of an acolyte or follower, but rather to draw lines of flight from Deleuze's thought and expand, rhizomatically, into new terrain. The schizoanalytical project, as exemplified in this collection, performs precisely this dynamic operation. The critics, academics and philosophers here presenting their readings of schizoanalysis of cinema are all embroiled in making Deleuze anew – finding points of contention, adaptation and combination that can spring forth into new epistemologies, ways of seeing and becoming. Although varying greatly in tone and approach, the eleven essays in this collection are all concerned with making new assemblages from the entirety of Deleuze and Guattari's work. Each author takes Deleuze's study of cinema on a new journey, via schizoanalysis, to address issues of how the experience of cinema can allow the schizo to become. Common strands in the collection include: (1) a focus on the socio-political context of filmic production; (2) the interaction between brain, screen and the social field that is formed by experiencing cinema; and (3) faciality and delirium as cinematic affects that express the schizo. Treating each strand in turn (place, space and face), I will examine each of the essays in the collection to explore how they apply and expand on Deleuze and Guattari's theory in order to perform specific actions of schizoanalysis.

Place

The combinations and incursions attempted within the collection are addressed, as Ian Buchanan indicates in the introduction, towards combining conceptual structures from different Deleuzian texts, particularly the use of schizoanalytical strictures from *Anti-Oedipus* and *A Thousand Plateaus* alongside Deleuze's taxonomy of cinematic images from *Cinema 1* and *Cinema 2*. Several of the contributors also highlight possible weaknesses in the cinema books, specifically addressing concerns with those texts' possible Euro-centrism and concentration on auteur 'high-culture' cinema. In *Cinema 1* and *Cinema 2*, Deleuze's ascetic and exclusive view of the majority of films was that they are null and void, in terms of political and philosophical value, due to their empty repetition. In this view, the true artist's task is to avoid the given, to avoid 'opinion' and stagnant, mediocre thought (thought and images that reinforce the molar aggregates). Buchanan relates this 'gelatinous morass of the given' to the process of commodification in late capitalism, wherein cinema's potential is subsumed into propaganda and a global conduit for interpellation, hegemony and heterogeneity. According to Deleuze, *auteurs* escape commodification by producing avant-garde, signature films that produce genuine differentiation and new lines of flight. Buchanan posits a reversal of this concentration on the molecular, to instead read the molar structure in order to ascertain how commodification is organised. This is schizoanalysis applied to understand the molar machine in order to better dismantle it, which is how Buchanan brings Deleuzian analysis to a point where any films, no matter how low-brow, can be examined through schizoanalysis for deconstructivist openings into new forms of thinking.

In 'Off Your Face: Schizoanalysis, Faciality and Film', Anna Powell makes her own incursion against the standard application of Deleuzian cinema theory to state that art-house cinema is 'pre-digested'. Auteur and experimental cinema challenges us with illogical cuts, a-temporality and non-linear narrative – but for Powell, this makes applying Deleuze and Guattari's theories to such films all too easy.

In contrast, popular cinema requires more work to deterritorialise, and examining mainstream science fiction and fantasy opens up the schizoanalysis of cinema to other possible lines of flight. In 'Schizoanalysis, Spectacle and the Spaghetti Western', David Martin-Jones addresses the spectacle of modern production and consumption of populist cinema. Referencing Rosie Thomas on Indian cinema and Tom Gunning on silent cinema, as well as Italian westerns produced in the latter part of the last century, Martin-Jones is particularly concerned with the schizoanalysis of the whole socio-political assemblage of cinema. Martin-Jones's essay uses *A Thousand Plateaus*' interactive planes to make a theoretical move to see movement and time-images as an interactive flow, as the linearity of movement-images is perpetually undermined by the virtuality of time-images. Martin-Jones views the time-image is an expression of the molecular, destabilising the molar. From this perspective, the cinema books are a formal taxonomy, but used in conjunction with schizoanalysis of *Anti Oedipus* and *A Thousand Plateaus*, image categories can be opened up to see how images, artefacts and historiographies all interact in re- and deterritorialising flows. Thus, schizoanalysis that takes into account context views cinema as striations, relevant to modes of production of its particular time and place, and its intentionality towards its audience.

With a similar concern for national context and modes of production, in 'Cinemas of Minor Frenchness', Bill Marshall addresses Quebecois cinema as specifically minor – that is, involved in de- and reterritorialisation through non-majoritarian positions of history, geography and language. Marshall states that social groups in these positions can reterritorialise in new language or seek a continual undermining of molar language. This proactive application and cross-fertilisation across Deleuze and Guattari's work is to be commended, allowing as it does for cinema to be considered truly outside of the realms of signification and representation, not only at the level of time-images but as an entire machinic assemblage, including socio-political contextual factors. This widens the depth and variety of types of cinematic genre and form that can be explored through a Deleuzian lens, and furthermore allows us to take cinematic experience as a conduit for the evocation and instantiation of post-structuralist modes of consciousness and agency.

Space

As well as allowing socio-political factors to be considered in relation to Deleuzian theory and cinema, schizoanalysis of cinema (where multiple aspects of Deleuze are applied to the cinematic experience) allow openings of how cinema can come to expose the non-human, post-subjective aspects of a Deleuzian schizo consciousness. Several of the authors in the collection pursue this line of flight. In 'Schizoanalysis and the Phenomenology of Cinema', Joe Hughes embarks upon a phenomenological comparative study across a range of Deleuze and Guattari's work in order to draw from them a reading of schizoanalysis as particularly relevant to the concerns of post-structuralist subjectivity. According to Hughes's interpretation of Deleuze, images are not abstract ideals but rather particular potentialities or instances in a particular 'material subject' (16). Hughes contends that Deleuze's taxonomy of cinema is thus not semiological but semiotic, describing not a language structure but a phenomenology. Hughes considers the congruence of phenomenological structures in *Logic of Sense* and *Anti-Oedipus* and further applies these parallels to the system of images described in *Cinema 1*, aligning the depictions of unconscious, passive synthesis to demonstrate that 'all three are accounts of the same Deleuzian unconscious' (25). Through the exposition of parallel structures across the work of Deleuze, Hughes establishes that all three texts are examples of schizoanalysis, describing a 'transcendental unconscious beginning with its ultimate elements' (26).

Mark Riley's 'Disorientation, Duration and Tarkovsky' addresses Andrey Tarkovsky's films *Solaris* (1972) and *Stalker* (1979) to reveal how schizoanalysis must come from drawing variant lines. As Deleuze and Guattari expose desire as machinic and performative, to break existing patterns requires that we partake in nomadic practice. Hence the schizoanalytical power of cinema is in its capacity for indetermination. Riley locates this power in cinema specifically to 'temporal de-coordination', this being the infarction of past into present and thus the virtual into the actual. Cinema is essentially de-coordinated in this way as it is specifically a recording of past experienced in a present. The experience of cinema illuminates that all perception is constituted in this way. The expression of virtuality into actuality is the constant becoming of experience and ultimately all experience is of this dynamic. For Riley, thought begins with an 'encounter with simulacrum' of individuality, but individuation is in fact a disguise or mask. What is experienced in the disorientation of Tarkovsky's cinema is the trace of the virtual that always accompanies phenomenological actuality.

Gregg Lambert's essay 'Schizoanalysis and the Cinema of the Brain' posits that brain and world have an interval, but not a separation. Deleuze's conception of brain function is non-Euclidean, accommodating synaptic gaps and gates that have random, changing connections. This framework correlates with the probability and uncertainty of quantum mechanics in the brain. Similarly, the time-image in cinema exposes quantum leaps of perception and apperception. Lambert illustrates this with reference to Stanley Kubrick's cinema: the delirium of General Ripper (*Dr. Strangelove*, 1964), The Overlook (*The Shining*, 1980) and HAL (*2001: A Space Odyssey*, 1968). The simultaneity of rational and irrational within the films is comparable to the uncertainty of the connection between brain and world. Kubrick's films, which incorporate simultaneity of delirium and the social fields that topographically locate that delirium, thus expose the schizoanalytical relation of multitudinous multiplicitous desire.

Patricia Pisters's 'Delirium Cinema or Machines of the Invisible?' draws its methodology from *Essays Critical and Clinical*. Pisters describes modern image abundance as 'madness'. Cinemas take place within this madness. Pisters uses Deleuze and Guattari's assessment of schizophrenia as a technique to draw philosophical value from immersion in cinematic delirium. Pisters differentiates between two strands of Deleuze and Guattari's treatment of schizophrenia. In *Anti-Oedipus*, we are advised of schizophrenisation, this being the movement and flow/process of de- and reterritorialisation. In *A Thousand Plateaus*, the figure of the schizophrenic is called upon to bring forth rhizomatics, the Body without Organs and Becoming. In both works, schizophrenia may be viewed as either process (breakthrough) or disease (breakdown). Pisters characterises the schizoanalytical project as bringing about a movement from cinema as 'machine of the visible' to 'machine of the invisible'. This is the move from representation and spectatorial interpretation, to brain/screen assemblage. Schizoanalysis is a 'new episteme' – prioritising choice and belief over knowledge.

In 'An Ethics of Spectatorship: Love, Death and Cinema', Patricia MacCormack takes these phenomenological analyses of the cinematic experience a stage further, to expose how we might go beyond mere subjective dissolution and even expressive creativity, into a specifically ethical relation with the world. MacCormack contends that representation, and its analysis through reading, 'massacre' the image. In the cinematic experience, any presumption of analytic understanding of the viewed images as objects of desire, to be resolved into representations, annihilates the Event of connectivity and being-with of the brain/screen assemblage. She states that ethics becomes impossible when interpretation becomes a quest to 'know'. Images cannot be desired as objects, to be understood as alterities, but must be directly absorbed into brain and body as integral to the forming of ourselves, viscera and thought combined. To suspend the assumption of subject/object divide between subjectivity and images is to enter a state of grace and 'we are gracious to cinema to the extent that we open up potentialities of thought without a compulsion to convert images to meaning for knowledge'. Such spectatorship, which allows images to be part of what we are, allows ethics as a love-relation between self, world and social formations.

Face

Continuing with the focus on non-subjective non-identitarian formations of singular consciousness, three essays in the collection address a specific focus to the issue of faciality in Deleuze's writings on cinema. In 'Suspended Gestures: Schizoanalysis, Affect and the Face in Cinema', Amy Herzog questions whether it is anomalous for Deleuze to relate faciality (specifically in Bergman's close-up shots) to a-linguistic, non-significatory expression of affect, given that (1) Deleuze is usually careful to avoid correlation between his taxonomic concepts and particular techniques and (2) Deleuze does not wish to reduce filmic expressions of affect to a communication to be psychologically interpreted. The face in close-up appears to attract both these eventualities, making Deleuze's concentration on Bergman seem, at first, to be problematic. This apparent anomaly is essentially set up as a straw man by Herzog, who goes on to explore the complexity of Deleuze's formulation of faciality, as it relates to the schizoanalytical project of dismantling ingrained assumptions and producing new traversals of the social field. Herzog explicates how the face is in fact integral to schizoanalysis by relating the affective force of faciality to the Bergsonian interval in perception wherein the inescapable residue of the virtual (and the durational) is found. The face, in evoking both immobility and motion, becomes the 'sheer potential' of the 'suspended gesture'. Herzog addresses Francis Bacon's paintings and Pedro Almodovar's *Bad Education* (2004) as illustrative of the ways that faciality can be harnessed by art to evoke new lines of flight away from subjectivity and expose the constructedness and violence of individuation.

Returning to 'Off Your Face: Schizoanalysis, Faciality and Film', we can see that Anna Powell finds facial mutation to be specifically schizoanalytical because the affect of participating in a cinematic experience where faciality is corroded and delirious becomes an infective, viral force that impacts directly upon our consciousness (as brain/screen assemblage).

In 'Losing Face', Gregory Flaxman and Elena Oxman address the idea of faciality in cinema through a Deleuzian analysis that imbues the face with non-interpretative affect. They state that 'the face renders thinking problematic'. Confronted with the face as ultimately unrecognisable, we are thrown into non-thought, non-philosophy: that which thought arises against. Flaxman and Oxman's elucidation of The Other Person communicates the variability, the 'assemblage of relations' of recognising an Other. The chicken and egg games of self/other priority are exposed as the ongoing expression of thought, of the virtual into the actual. This moves past Kantian processional perception to remove exteriority/internality and replace it with intensity and extensity within variable parameters of contextual relation. Thus, the possible is not predicated as that which can be understood; what can be understood forms as experience out of our relations with the possible (the virtual). Cinema (in close-up) takes the face apart (from the body). Affection writes itself across the face as expressions pass in flux, fluctuating as passion. The affection-image short-circuits translation and representation, expressing instead a direct form of agency. Affect here becomes as expression that is without actualisation, as opposed to linguistically based interpretation that forms fixed identity and a personhood ascribed to that face particularly. The affection-image is thus shown by Flaxman and Oxman to escape the socio-political encoding of the face in modern culture, allowing for a radical reimagining of subjectivity as non-human, imperceptible and faceless.

As with schizoanalysis of cinema's concern for the analysis and deterritorialisation of molar aggregates, the value of using the schizo-analytical elements of Deleuze and Guattari's theories in reference to the phenomenological Event of cinematic experience is very clear. Through cinema – through the time-image and its exposure of Duration and the Bergsonian gap of singularity as non-subjective consciousness – we can find a way to a post-structuralist ethics where care and love replace the phantoms of rationality and representation. This is an active, radical epistemology that produces multiple possibilities for new ways of engaging as singularities with societal structure and control. This conception places all forms of art at the heart of becoming, without isolating it in any way as a purely aesthetic practice. From the schizoanalysis of cinema as a phenomenology with necessarily ethical results, the category of aesthetics become enmeshed with affect, which in turn is enmeshed entirely in what enjoins consciousness with the flux of multiplicitous becoming. From this position, art and participation in art (of any kind) is always potentially radical when we engage in its Event as a schizo becoming. This collection is thus not just valuable to cinema studies. It also opens up avenues for engaging with wider issues about other art forms such as schizoanalysis of genres of literature, for one, and with ethical questions regarding how to engage, post-structurally, with global exploitation and greed, for another. The collection also raises the issue of how to write Deleuze: analytically and academically or poetically? The structures and strictures of academic writing preclude the rhizomatic, which might be better expressed in music or non-representational art. In the same way that the authors in the collection make a stand, in the spirit of Deleuze, against strict interpretation of his theories, and call instead towards combination, expansion and the advantages of delirium, we may consider if it is appropriate to write on Deleuze, more as Deleuze would push us to write. Patricia MacCormack achieves this, writing with huge passion and immersion in her subject and having the becoming of the thought express itself out of the pattern as much as the content of the words. This is another opening that could be made, from schizoanalysis of cinema and art, to schizoanalysis of what it means to write academically about Deleuze. The collection of essays titled *Deleuze and the Schizoanalysis of Cinema* may be said, then, to be an Event that has molecular potential far beyond the usual conception of writing about cinema, or Deleuze.

Helen Darby
Manchester Metropolitan University
DOI: 10.3366/dls.2013.0108

Contributors

Éric Alliez is Professor of Contemporary French Philosophy at Kingston University and a Professor at the University of Paris 8. His work centres on contemporary philosophy and contemporary art. His most recent books include *The Guattari Effect* (2011), edited with Andrew Goffey; *L'Oeil-Cerveau: nouvelles histoires de la peinture moderne* (2007), co-authored with J.-C. Martin; and *La Pensée-Matisse: portrait de l'artiste en hyperfauve* (2005), co-authored with J.-C. Bonne.

Benoît Dillet is a PhD candidate in Politics and Government at the University of Kent. He is the editor, with Iain MacKenzie and Robert Porter, of the *Edinburgh Companion to Poststructuralism* (forthcoming 2013). Email: B.Dillet@kent.ac.uk.

Jean-Claude Dumoncel teaches logic and natural philosophy. His work centres on the relation between analytic philosophy and the Bergsonian legacy as represented by Deleuze and illustrated by Proust. This line of investigation has brought him to study the common confines of the mathematical theory of categories and modal logic, especially as it is developed in the work of A. N. Prior, which leads to hybrid logic and its @ operator. Along with books on Whitehead and Wittgenstein, his most recent publications include *Philosophie des mathématiques* (2002), *La Philosophie telle quelle* (2004) and *Deleuze face à face* (2009).

Craig Lundy is a Research Fellow in the Institute for Social Transformation Research at the University of Wollongong. He is the author of *History and Becoming: Deleuze's Philosophy of Creativity* (2012) and of various papers on European philosophy.

Daniela Voss completed her PhD at the Free University of Berlin in 2011. She is the author of *Deleuze and the Transcendental Conditions of Thought* (forthcoming 2013). Her research interests focus on French post-structuralism, and Kantian and post-Kantian philosophy.

Deleuze Studies 7.2 (2013): 298
DOI: 10.3366/dls.2013.0109
© Edinburgh University Press
www.euppublishing.com/dls

Call for Papers

Deleuze. Guattari. Schizoanalysis. Education.
Where: Murdoch University, Perth, Australia
When: Monday 9ᵗʰ December–Wednesday 11ᵗʰ December 2013
Abstracts Due: Monday 29ᵗʰ July 2013
Convener: Greg Thompson Greg.Thompson@murdoch.edu.au

> We're in the midst of a general breakdown of all sites of
> confinement – prisons, hospitals, schools, families. The family
> is an "interior" that's breaking down like all other interiors –
> educational, professional and so on. (...) Educational reforms,
> industrial reforms, hospital, army, prison reforms; but everyone
> knows these institutions are more or less in terminal decline. (...) It
> is not a question of worrying or hoping for the best, but of finding
> new weapons.
>
> Gilles Deleuze, "Postscript on Control Societies" p. 178

This conference is designed for theorists and practitioners working at
the intersection of Deleuze, Guattari, Schizoanalysis and Education to
share their work. We welcome papers addressing a broad range of issues
relating to institutional education such as schools, universities, technical
colleges and other institutions of higher education. We also welcome papers
addressing the use of Deleuze, Guattari and their combined works in
areas typically associated with mainstream education including pedagogy,
teaching, learning, teacher education, theories of self, subjectivity, the space
and time of the classroom and so on. Those working outside what may
be termed mainstream education in alternative education contexts are also
encouraged to participate.

Potential themes

- Education space-time
- Feminisms/Feminist theory and education
- Psychoanalytic theory and Education
- Schizoanalysis and Education
- Affect and Education
- Identity, faciality, education
- Geophilosophy and education
- De-/Re-/Territorialisation and Education
- Education, modulation and control societies
- Multiplicities and education
- Practical applications of Deleuze and Guattari's ideas in educational
  settings
- And then... and then... and then...

For further information go to the Conference website
http://www.murdoch.edu.au/School-of-Education/Research/Deleuze-
Conference-2013/

Printed and bound by CPI Group (UK) Ltd, Croydon, CR0 4YY

14/03/2025

01833346-0011